# How Do We Talk About Abortion?

# How Do We Talk About Abortion?

*A Feminist Pastoral Theology*

Emma Percy

**scm press**

© Emma Percy 2025

Published in 2025 by SCM Press

Editorial office
3rd Floor, Invicta House,
110 Golden Lane,
London EC1Y 0TG, UK

www.scmpress.co.uk

SCM Press is an imprint of Hymns Ancient & Modern Ltd
(a registered charity)

Hymns Ancient & Modern® is a registered trademark of
Hymns Ancient & Modern Ltd
13A Hellesdon Park Road, Norwich,
Norfolk NR6 5DR, UK

All rights reserved. No part of this publication may be reproduced,
stored in a retrieval system, or transmitted,
in any form or by any means, electronic, mechanical,
photocopying or otherwise, without the prior permission of
the publisher, SCM Press.

The Author has asserted her right under the Copyright, Designs and
Patents Act 1988 to be identified as the Author of this Work

Scripture quotations are from New Revised Standard Version Bible:
Anglicized Edition, copyright © 1989, 1995 National Council of the
Churches of Christ in the United States of America. Used by permission.
All rights reserved worldwide.

British Library Cataloguing in Publication data

A catalogue record for this book is available
from the British Library

ISBN: 978-0-334-06570-8

EU GPSR Authorised Representative
LOGOS EUROPE, 9 rue Nicolas Poussin, 17000, LA ROCHELLE, France
E-mail: Contact@logoseurope.eu

No part of this book may be used or reproduced in any manner for the
purpose of training artificial intelligence technologies or systems.

Typeset by Regent Typesetting

# Contents

*Acknowledgements* vii

Introduction: How Do We Talk About Abortion? ix

1 A Problem of Sex 1
2 Abortion and Contraception: Changing Attitudes 26
3 Unintended Pregnancy and Early Abortion 54
4 Prenatal Diagnosis and Abortion 79
5 How Do We Talk Pastorally About Abortion? 113

Conclusion 134

*Select Bibliography* 142
*Index of Bible References* 145
*Index of Names and Subjects* 147

# Acknowledgements

I would like to thank Virginia Theological Seminary and St Mary's Episcopal Church of Arlington, Virginia, for awarding me a Merrow Fellowship in autumn 2022. Particular thanks go to the Dean, The Very Revd Ian Markham, the Revd Melody Knowles and Revd Andrew Merrow. My time in Virginia enabled me to work on the early stages of this book. My colleagues at the Divinity Department of Aberdeen University have supported and encouraged me, even when some disagree with my views. Thanks go to the postgraduate students, especially the practical theologians, for good conversations and making me so welcome. Particular thanks go to Dr Henna Cundill for help both in thinking and in managing computer glitches. Thanks go to all of those currently working in this difficult field of theology, not least Margeret Kamitsuka who shared her wisdom and encouragement. As always, thanks go to Martyn who never fails to believe in me.

# Introduction
# How Do We Talk About Abortion?

How do we talk about abortion? The answer for many people is that they would rather not. It is a contentious issue, and although many people hold a position on the topic, they would prefer not to get into an argument. Yet, others do talk about it. For some, abortion is an issue they do want to talk about because they view it as a practice that is wrong. Many anti-abortion campaigners come from a position of faith and see abortion as a sin. Others want to stress women's bodily autonomy, and challenge those who seek to make decisions on behalf of women about their pregnant bodies. These positions have become political and polemical. Abortion is discussed by those who make laws that place limits on how, when and why women can access safe abortion procedures. It is also discussed by ethicists, religious and secular, considering if, and in what circumstances, an abortion decision is morally justifiable. Meanwhile, women have abortions. They have them safely in countries where there is access to good medical care, and less safely in countries where the practice is illegal or prohibitively expensive. It seems that sometimes women find themselves pregnant and decide that for many reasons they do not want to be pregnant and do not want to bring a child into their life at this time, in these circumstances.

This book aims to complexify thinking around abortion to show that it is not a simple matter of being pro- or anti-abortion, pro- or anti-choice, pro- or anti-life. The reality is that most people already have a nuanced view that is heavily contextual.

# HOW DO WE TALK ABOUT ABORTION?

The National Centre for Social Research has been tracking attitudes to abortion in Britain since 1983. The most recent report shows strong support for abortion: 95% of people believe abortion should be allowed if the woman's health is seriously endangered by the pregnancy, and 89% if there is a strong chance of the baby having a serious health condition. The attitudes are slightly less emphatic when finances drive the decision, or when the woman chooses not to have the child with no reason given. However, the figures still show that the majority support women's decisions. Even in the scenario of an unmarried woman who chooses not to marry and not to have the child, 68% support her right to make that decision. When religious faith is factored into the responses, it makes a difference. On the question of whether abortion is acceptable if the woman on her own decides not to have the child, 84% of those with no religious affiliation replied yes. Although the figures drop when religious affiliation is included, the same question receives an affirmative response from 58% of those identifying as Roman Catholic and 62%–72% of adherents to other religions. So, even within Catholicism, which holds a very public anti-abortion position, there appears to be a recognition of the complexity of contextual abortion decisions and a sense that women have the right to make them. The report concludes that more than half of individuals from each religious background express support for abortion in all scenarios.[1]

These survey findings seem contrary to the public perception of religious views. Many assume that all Christians are opposed to abortion. In their recent study of Catholic attitudes to abortion in Britain, Lowe and Page note that, although the majority hold nuanced, contextually permissive attitudes, there was no space for discussing abortion in this way because it was a taboo topic and one likely to cause contention. 'This meant that while participants often had a contextual view of abortion – that it was more acceptable in certain situations, but not in others – this was not typically discussed.'[2] Public statements from an anti-abortion position may be expressed from the pulpit, in prayers, through leaflets placed at the back

# INTRODUCTION

of church, etc., but a more permissive position is hidden. Lowe and Page note that this is not just an issue in Catholicism: 'Discussing abortion in public contexts is not straightforward ... abortion is stigmatized, not just within religious contexts but secular ones too, which results in a lack of open discussion and silencing.'[3] This has pastoral consequences. It makes it less likely for women to turn to religious leaders and pastors for support in making abortion decisions or in reflecting on them after the event. It also makes it less likely for women to turn to their church community for support. This is particularly true when the language of sin and repentance is used in the way Churches talk about abortion.

This inability to talk about abortion in a nuanced way impacts access to religious pastoral care. Clergy tend to have limited experience and lack training in discussing abortion decisions. This can mean they perpetuate misconceptions and provide misinformation. The language used in formal Church statements on the issue and by those who campaign against abortion includes ideas of sin, judgement, tragedy and repentance. This can prejudge women's experiences and lead to feelings of guilt, even when the woman believes she made the right decision. Where there is a permissive view of abortion, it is usually described as exceptional, leading to unhelpful categorizing of acceptable and unacceptable circumstances: tragic abortion decisions as opposed to selfish ones. Silence allows stigma to continue. While those who terminate a pregnancy for a foetal anomaly may receive pastoral care and options of rituals to mark the loss, assumptions about other abortion decisions mean that there is less likely to be provision to mark an ending and to entrust what has been lost to God's mercy. The limited liturgical resources offered around abortion presume the need for repentance.

## Not talking about abortion

The statistics show that as many as one in three women in the UK will have an abortion during their reproductive life.[4] This means that in most congregations, there will be some women who have made an abortion decision. Yet, pastoral experience of talking to women about this is very limited. In my own pastoral ministry of over 30 years, I have had very few conversations with women who have had an abortion or were considering one, despite being known to have liberal views on social issues. Most of the conversations I have had concerned issues of prenatal foetal anomalies. In a study of ministers from mainline Protestant churches in Georgia, USA, despite their holding a wide range of views on abortion, most had little to no experience of supporting someone pastorally on this issue.[5] I suspect that this would be true if a similar study were conducted in UK churches. Where the topic is discussed, it is more likely to be abstract discussions about the rights and wrongs of abortion – discussions that have not been informed by lived experience. On many contentious topics, pastoral wisdom is honed through listening to the lives of those who have faced concrete situations. This is why practical theology stresses the importance of listening to lived experience in recognizing the complexity of people's lives. This can challenge assumptions held about how and why people make the decisions they do. The lack of pastoral conversations about abortion means that it is hard to develop nuanced understanding and all too easy to let assumptions about the kind of people who have abortions go unchallenged. It also means that certain myths can be perpetuated.

The study of the ministers in Georgia concluded that 'several misperceptions regarding abortion underlie religious leaders' attitudes, beliefs, and pastoral care practices and run counter to existing scientific evidence'.[6] The key misperception was that women suffer poor mental health as a result of having an abortion; this is sometimes referred to as 'post-abortion syndrome'. The study states 'many pastors described the adverse

## INTRODUCTION

psychological effects of having an abortion including spiritual questioning, guilt, and lifelong emotional struggle and pain. In contrast, 30 years of research – including studies that measured mental and emotional distress before pregnancy – suggest legal induced abortion does not pose significant mental health risks for women.' This misperception has been exacerbated by anti-abortion organizations, many of which are Christian. Alongside the concerns for the unborn has been the argument that abortion harms the woman as well. Not only is it often suggested that women's mental health will suffer, but claims of links to breast cancer, future ectopic pregnancy or infertility are made without any evidence. For those who have not talked to women who have had an abortion, or have not read material on the subject, it can be all too easy to think there is substance in the claim that abortions negatively affect the women who have them. It may also be that those who do turn to Church leaders for pastoral support about abortion decisions, especially those made in the past, do so because of the espoused view of most Churches that abortion is sinful or even, if not sinful, tragic. This means they may reinforce the idea that abortion leaves women with unresolved guilt.

In their study of Roman Catholic parishes in the UK, Lowe and Page found that priests were unlikely to be approached by a parishioner to talk about an abortion decision. The Church's views are clear, and the priest would be obliged to counsel that abortion is considered a serious sin. 'This meant that priests' encounters with parishioners' abortion stories were often concentrated on cases where the abortion had occurred historically, but where the parishioner still retained negative feelings.'[7] Even in Church denominations where the stance on abortion is less clear cut, the language of regret and repentance is often present. It may therefore be difficult for women to simply say that they made the right decision and that they are grateful for the procedure. Yet, extensive research suggests that this is how the majority of women feel. The consensus of research shows that the experience of having an abortion does not lead to long-term mental health problems. The predominant response to an abortion is relief.⁸ A difficult experience such as an abortion might exacerbate pre-existing mental health issues. However, there is no evidence that the fact of having an abortion has a negative lasting impact on a woman's mental health.

A 2020 study from the USA considering woman's attitudes from before and over the five years following an abortion found that 97% felt they had made the right decision one week after the abortion. This rose to 99% five years after the abortion. They found no evidence of emergent negative or positive emotions over the period. Among the women who had found the abortion decision very or somewhat difficult, there were initially more negative emotions, but these had levelled out over five years to be consistent with those who did not find the decision difficult.⁹ This was also true for those who noted high levels of community abortion stigma. However, they note: 'Results suggest that sociocultural context is important for women's post-abortion assessment of their abortion decision.'¹⁰ The circumstances that led to the abortion, if complex or traumatic, might lead to ongoing distress. It may be particularly difficult for women to talk about their sense of rightness about an abortion decision if they presume that this would be counter to a Christian view that it was a tragedy or a grave sin. It is also clear that an internalized or externalized strong disapproval of abortion can result in feelings of guilt. Are those who do turn to the church for pastoral support expressing a sense of guilt, unease or regret, doing so because this is the only language the church is offering them? If so, it is important for those who have a pastoral role to recognize the validity of the research that shows that post-abortion stress and long-term mental health problems consequent on an abortion decision are rare.

The people who often do not talk about abortion are the women who have them. Stigma and fear of judgement silence women's experience, and that is particularly true in religious settings. This book is written from a pastoral perspective. It takes as a given the fact that abortions happen and that the decision to terminate is made by women who find themselves in a situation they would rather not be in. Nobody aspires to

## INTRODUCTION

have an abortion; it is a response to a particular set of circumstances. Women may find the decision anything between straightforward or extremely difficult, but it will always be a concrete decision. Some women may think that they would never have an abortion and find themselves deciding to do so in this situation. Other women may assume that they would terminate a pregnancy and then find they choose not to.

As well as being pastoral, this book is written from a feminist perspective. Abortion decisions are made by women because the costly process of gestating a human life is an embodied female experience. Once a woman commits to a pregnancy, then it is hers alone; she cannot share the gestation with anyone else or take a break. Through pregnancy and childbirth, she becomes a mother to this baby with all the ramifications of such a relationship.

In foregrounding women, I am already taking a position. On a recent holiday, I picked up a leaflet from a church café produced by a Christian organization opposed to abortion. This leaflet never once mentioned that a woman was involved. The drawing of a free-floating foetus was not contained in a woman's body. To talk about pregnancy and the gestation of a human life without talking about women should be impossible. A woman is not simply a container within which a fertilized ovum moves from the earliest cell divisions to a full-term baby. She gestates this emerging life, enabling this to happen through the generous sharing of her body. It is costly work. It can place her at risk, leaving her with short- or long-term health problems. Women still die from the complications of pregnancy and childbirth. Pregnancy is also precarious. Discussions of deliberate pregnancy endings need to be situated within the reality of spontaneous pregnancy loss. It is estimated that one in five pregnancies ends spontaneously. The reality of human reproduction is unfair. Those who want children may struggle with infertility, miscarriage and loss. Those who do not want children can find themselves pregnant at the wrong time, with the wrong person or in the wrong situation.

The topic of abortion is considered from legal, medical and

ethical perspectives. This involves considering the rights of the emerging life and often discusses questions of personhood. Theological concerns about when human life begins and God's role in conception have shaped principled positions on when abortion might be morally acceptable or not. Margaret Kamitsuka explores the historical and current theological discussions of abortion in *Abortion in the Christian Tradition*.[11] I am indebted to her careful scholarship. Legislation, moral arguments and Church rules have all in different ways sought to limit or eradicate abortion, and yet women still seek out ways to end certain pregnancies. Where safe abortion is not an option because of legislation, affordability or other access issues, then women turn to folk remedies or unsafe interventions. They risk their own lives in doing so. As a pastoral response, I am less interested in discussing the principle of abortion, instead focusing on understanding the reasons why and questioning how to support those who make such decisions.

An important aspect of good pastoral conversations about complex issues involves recognizing the embedded theology each person brings. In their book *How to Think Theologically*, Stone and Duke state:

> Christians learn what faith is all about from countless daily encounters with their Christianity – formal and informal, planned and unplanned. This understanding of faith, disseminated by the church and assimilated by its members in their daily lives, will be called embedded theology.[12]

When people have life crises or encounters with those who see God differently, this embedded theology can make it hard to navigate both life and faith. Good pastoral conversations can help examine these unexamined theological ideas and move towards what Stone and Duke call 'deliberative theology'. They note that:

> it is embedded theology that rushes to the frontline in every battle over the moral and social issues of the day. Christians

rise up to defend their theological convictions or express outrage when those convictions are threatened. Turn on the evening news and witness the two sides of the abortion question facing off: even their placards testify to their differing embedded understandings of faith.[13]

Thus, in order to have good pastoral conversations about abortion, aspects of embedded theology need to be examined.

Those reflecting theologically on issues of infertility and miscarriage have already begun this work. Karen O'Donnell's work in this area has been groundbreaking, showing how theology must pay attention to the realities of reproductive loss. In her book *The Dark Womb*,[14] she challenges a theology of providence that maintains God ordains each conception. Such a theology is deeply problematic in the light of infertility and miscarriage. It is also problematic in thinking about unintended pregnancies, and especially those that are a result of forced or coerced sexual encounters. These insights mean that care needs to be taken in the use of Scripture. The stories and metaphors of barrenness and fertility that see God as the one who opens and shuts wombs require sensitive interpretation. The way that this language focuses on women and their bodies is often deeply problematic. The poetic references to life in the womb also need careful interpretation. It is possible to have a theological understanding of God's care for all aspects of life without presuming that God directs each conception and has a specific plan for each beginning. There are too many spontaneous pregnancy losses, and it is hard to believe that this is intentional. Recognizing the unfairness of human reproduction challenges embedded assumptions that maintain that each conception will or must proceed to birth. This is an issue for abortion, and for IVF and other procedures where embryos exist outside of the womb.

Theological reflection on reproductive loss also challenges traditional views about women's nature and purpose. Not everyone will be a mother; not everyone will procreate. Enriching the understanding of women's creativity beyond the specifically maternal requires unsettling traditional ideas about women's nature and God's 'design' for sexual difference. This leads to questions about sex and sexuality, the place of sexual desire and the purpose of sex.

Chapter 1 will give a brief overview of the Christian traditions' valorizing of sexual continence and virginity. The idea that sexual intercourse was for procreation, not for sexual pleasure, shaped a theology that connected sex to sin and shame. When the Reformers challenged the prioritizing of celibacy, they recognized that sexual pleasure could strengthen the marital relationship. Yet, sex outside of marriage was sinful and publicly punished. Women's behaviour has traditionally been controlled, and women who fall have been judged as sinners regardless of whether they were raped, seduced or willingly participated in sex outside of marriage. Attitudes to women who have abortions are often shaped by these theological traditions. The spoken or unspoken assumption that a woman should face the consequences of her behaviour means that she should continue an unintended pregnancy and make provision for her child. Recognizing that theologies of sex have rarely considered women's sexual desires needs to prompt further theological reflection that might have something positive to say in today's world.

Abortion has often been portrayed as a negation of motherhood. Clearly, an abortion means deciding not to bring to birth a child whose mother you will be. Yet, I follow Kamitsuka in seeing abortion as a maternal decision. It involves the woman considering all that would be needed to be this potential child's mother and deciding that at this time, in these circumstances, this is not a commitment she can make. In doing so, abortion decisions draw on ideas of maternal responsibility, recognizing the seriousness of these demands.

Chapter 2 will look at the history of contraception and abortion. It will explore the part that the Church of England and the Anglican Communion played in the acceptance of contraception. This developed into a wider protestant theology of responsible parenting, where the Christian duty of prudence meant planning family size to suit resources. The assumption here is that there is a moral duty to think about what a child needs when thinking about bringing one into the world. The Church of England also played a part in the move to legalize abortion in the UK. The concern at the deaths and injuries sustained through illegal abortions motivated legalization to reduce harm. There was also a genuine concern for those women who felt that they had had enough children and who were struggling to manage with meagre resources.

Leslie Reagan, the historian of abortion legislation in the USA, notes that in Europe and the UK, feminist socialists were the lead campaigners for legalizing abortion. They were motivated by issues of inequality. Those with money could access discreet private abortions performed by doctors in appropriate settings. It was those without means who resorted to folk remedies and back-street abortionists, too often resulting in serious damage or loss of life. There were also inequalities in access to contraception and sexual education. Legalized abortion on the NHS alongside free access to contraception would help women of all backgrounds make responsible decisions about how many children they had and when they had them. The eventual legalization of abortion in the USA was shaped by a different language: feminist concerns for rights and bodily autonomy. In discussions of abortion, this rights language has become prominent. This leads to discussions of competing rights between the developing life in the womb and the woman's life, which play out in pro-life/pro-choice binaries. This binary is unhelpful. Focusing on maternal thinking and questions of parental and family responsibilities recognize the complexity of the moral decision being made, in which thought is given to the needs of the mother and the potential child.

The complexity of how to speak about the life developing in the womb is impacted by taking seriously women's experience of pregnancy and of pregnancy endings. The medical language of embryo and foetus is rarely how women speak, although the rise of fertility treatments means that the term 'embryo' is much more widely used. Thinking pastorally about pregnancy loss, both spontaneous and deliberate, means navigating language about what is lost. Writing about abortion in legal, medical and ethical contexts involves questions of foetal personhood and at what point in gestation particular rights should be afforded to the emerging life. In this book I do not engage in those debates. As a piece of pastoral theology, I am focusing on the fact that women have different ways of speaking about the life they are gestating.

Women relate differently to the experience of being pregnant. Some confirm their pregnancy very early; others come to realize slightly slower. Some have been planning for their baby for a long time; others conceive easily or unexpectedly. This may be the first, or a pregnancy after a loss or a second, third or further pregnancy. Women may be tentative about investing in their pregnancy for any number of reasons, or they may have confidently spoken of their baby from the earliest confirmation. When the pregnancy ends early through spontaneous or deliberate loss, then women will speak about the loss in the language they find most helpful. It is deeply important for some to grieve the loss of their baby even in the very early weeks of pregnancy, while others will use different terminology or even struggle to know how to speak of what they have lost. This holds true for those who terminate a pregnancy. They may end the life of the baby they feel unable to have or the beginning that should not have happened. Writing about her experience of being a patient advocate in an abortion clinic, Jeannie Ludlow explains how she learned to speak in the language that the client used. She titles her article 'Sometimes It's a Child and a Choice',[15] pointing out that women who have abortions may speak about this baby that they cannot have.

For the most part I will speak about the foetus, even though I acknowledge that it is not a term many women use. I will also talk about the 'developing life' or the 'emerging life'. Abortion is a deliberate ending of a life, and it is important to acknowledge that. Yet, this life is developing and has not yet been born. It is entirely contingent on the mother's body and

# INTRODUCTION

does not have a separate existence yet. The coming into being of a human life through being gestated in a woman's body is a unique experience without any equivalence. Between 80 and 90% of abortions happen before 10 weeks of pregnancy; many of these are medically induced, resembling a spontaneous miscarriage at this stage of pregnancy. Increasingly, these can be managed at home. In Chapter 3, I consider the unintended pregnancy and the decision to terminate. While acknowledging that unintended pregnancies can arise out of consensual, joyful sex, it is also important to recognize concerns about consent. Contraception failure, including the failure to use it or to use it properly, also plays a part in unintended pregnancies. Suggesting that a pregnancy should be continued in circumstances where consent was not given or was ambiguous, where contraception failed or the man refused to use it, places the full burden onto the woman. Even when the sex is consensual, is a consent to sex also a potential consent to pregnancy?

Later abortions arise when women take longer to make a decision, discover their pregnancy later, face changed circumstances or respond to health issues for themselves or for the foetus. They can also happen where there is difficulty accessing safe, free or affordable abortion. Under UK law, abortion is allowed on the grounds of a prenatal diagnosis of foetal anomalies. As these are often detected through prenatal scans and tests, they account for a proportion of abortions beyond the first trimester. The capacity to test for different genetic anomalies is increasing. Women and their partners already find themselves navigating complex issues of risk and potential with regard to a future child. The process of testing for certain conditions and offering abortion where there is a diagnosis raises concerns about the valuing of people living with these conditions. The medical setting of diagnosis and termination means that, in the eyes of the general public and in Christian communities, these abortions are viewed differently to those for unintended pregnancy. They may be seen as exceptional. Yet, they can add to the stigma around disability. Chapter 4 will consider these abortions.

## HOW DO WE TALK ABOUT ABORTION?

The final chapter will explore some of the pastoral responses to abortion. It will look at how misinformation can perpetuate abortion myths and inappropriate advice. It will discuss the language of sin, both individual and systemic. It will also consider the issue of rituals and prayers that might be appropriate to honour what is lost. The aim of the book is not to be prescriptive. It is to promote better conversations about abortion and the circumstances around such decisions. Research shows that religious disapproval can exacerbate abortion stigma. However, religious faith does not stop women having abortions; it simply makes it unlikely they will ask for help in integrating their faith and their lived experience. Focusing on the wider systemic issues of inequality, on the lack of support for people with disabilities, on poor sex education and on poor power dynamics between men and women, boys and girls, could all play a part in reducing abortions. When a woman finds herself in a situation where a pregnancy has begun that she does not want or does not feel able to continue, then access to a safe abortion can be her best option. The predominant response of women to an abortion is relief. Expecting or mandating a woman to continue a pregnancy will be deeply costly, profoundly changing her life; recognizing that must be part of any conversation about abortion.

In foregrounding women, I am aware that I am using a gendered term that excludes the trans men who can have children and who may find themselves making an abortion decision. Having considered the option of following some colleagues in speaking about pregnant persons, I have decided to continue to speak about women. I do so because I maintain that attitudes towards women in the history and tradition of the Church need to be considered in developing better conversations around sex and reproduction. A neutral term has benefits of inclusion, yet it can unwittingly obscure attitudes that have shaped, and continue to shape, responses to matters of pregnancy and abortion. Attitudes to abortion decisions contain within them ideas about women's sexual behaviour, their nature and their capacity to make reasoned decisions. Within Christian discus-

## INTRODUCTION

sions, these are all impacted by presumptions of God's creative design of men and women, of human reproduction and human pleasure.

Maintaining that abortion decisions can be both understandable and reasonable can sometimes be read as implying judgements on those who are living as the result of the opposite decision about a pregnancy. In a recent discussion about abortion after a conception as a result of rape, I was told about a wonderful woman who had been conceived in such circumstances. Was my stance on abortion after rape suggesting that she should not have existed? No: a distinction must be made between the moral value of a developing life and the moral value of the lived life. It is natural for us to project that value backwards, but it is also problematic and potentially reductionist. I joyfully acknowledge that remarkable people exist who are not shaped by how they were conceived. There are so many factors that shape who we are and the kinds of people we become; who we are is not programmed from the point of conception. Our genetic makeup may be decided early, but how those genes are expressed, how we develop as a human being, is not so deterministic. That valued individuals exist whose conception was through forced sex does not change the fact that rape is a violation, and expecting a woman to continue a pregnancy after rape can be a further form of violation and abuse. There are no guarantees that in continuing the pregnancy, a wonderful person will result. Even if it does, this might require considerable sacrifices on the part of the woman.

While rape is an extreme example, retrospective valuing is used to generally suggest that continuing a pregnancy is the better option. I am married to a man born in 1962 in a home for unmarried mothers and adopted at six weeks old. We do not know if his birth mother would have opted for an abortion had they been legal (the law legalizing abortion was passed in 1967 in the UK), but the fact that, though contacted, she has chosen not to meet him makes me think it would have been likely. From the perspective of many years of marriage, I love this man who is also the father of my children. He has done much good in the world. Had she terminated the pregnancy, he would not have existed. Yet, on one level he should not have existed in the first place because his birth father was cheating on his wife and young child, behaviour that I, and the Church, would condemn. Now the idea of his non-existence is impossible to comprehend, but I know there are many other aspects of his and my life that could have meant we would never have met or that we would have been very different people. Our lives are full of choices and happenstance; they are impacted by the decisions of others and by wider social circumstances. Any of us could have had a different life. To argue against the possibility of terminating a pregnancy from the reality of a known person is a specious argument. So to end a pregnancy is to end a life before it has been lived; it is not to pass judgement on the lives of the living.

## Notes

1 'How Are Attitudes towards Abortion in Britain Changing?', National Centre for Social Research (blog), https://natcen.ac.uk/how-are-attitudes-towards-abortion-britain-changing, accessed 11.04.2025.

2 Sarah-Jane Page and Pam Lowe, 2024, *Abortion and Catholicism in Britain: Attitudes, Lived Religion and Complexity*, Palgrave Studies in Lived Religion and Societal Challenges, Cham, Switzerland: Palgrave Macmillan, p. 226.

3 Page and Lowe, 2024, p. 101.

4 'My Body My Life', https://www.mybody-mylife.org/, accessed 11.04.2025.

5 Jessica L. Dozier et al., 'Abortion Attitudes, Religious and Moral Beliefs, and Pastoral Care among Protestant Religious Leaders in Georgia', ed. Jonathan Jong, *PLOS ONE* 15(7) (2020): e0235971, https://doi.org/10.1371/journal.pone.0235971, accessed 11.04.2025.

6 Dozier et al., 'Abortion Attitudes'.

7 Page and Lowe, *Abortion and Catholicism in Britain*, p. 134.

8 Corinne H. Rocca et al., 2020, 'Emotions and Decision Rightness over Five Years Following an Abortion: An Examination of Decision Difficulty and Abortion Stigma', *Social Science & Medicine* 248(4), March, p. 4, https://doi.org/10.1016/j.socscimed.2019.112704, accessed 11.04.2025.

9 Rocca et al., 'Emotions', p. 7.

10 Rocca et al., 'Emotions', p. 7.

11 Margaret D. Kamitsuka, 2019, *Abortion and the Christian Tradition: A Pro-Choice Theological Ethic*, Louisville, Kentucky: Westminster John Knox Press.

12 Howard W. Stone and James O. Duke, 2013, *How to Think Theologically*, 3rd edn, Augsburg: Fortress, p. 15, https://doi.org/10.2307/j.ctt22nmb9s, accessed 11.04.2025.

13 Stone and Duke, p. 17.

14 Karen O'Donnell, 2022, *Dark Womb: Re-Conceiving Theology through Reproductive Loss*, London: SCM Press.

15 Jeannie Ludlow, 2008, 'Sometimes It's a Child and a Choice: Toward an Embodied Abortion Praxis', *NWSA Journal* 20(1), Spring, pp. 26–50.

# I

# A Problem of Sex

Talking about abortion requires thinking about sex. The decision to terminate arises because a sexual encounter has resulted in a pregnancy. Attitudes to the permissiveness of abortion are shaped by attitudes to sexual behaviour, especially when the behaviour is deemed promiscuous. In a survey of abortion attitudes, Jelen concluded that the strongest correlation to an anti-abortion position was a disapproval of premarital sex.[1] The idea that a woman should face the consequences, if her sexual encounter leads to an unplanned conception, highlights the unequal burden of reproduction on women's lives. Women's sexual behaviour has historically been more heavily policed than men's and, despite the reality of seduction, coercion and rape, their 'fall' from chastity has been more heavily judged. Assumptions about women's natural, or God-designed, capacity for motherhood means that women are expected to love and care for any children they have, while men can choose which children they recognize as their own. An abortion decision is seen as a rejection of the maternal capacity to care and is thus unwomanly.

While studying sociology at university, my son was set an essay that became the most widely talked about assignment in his social group: 'Is heterosexual sex inherently oppressive to women?' He was initially indignant at the idea, yet his reading and reflection left him slightly disturbed and leaning towards an affirmative answer. This chapter will begin by noting the inherent inequality in human reproduction, which means that women's role in procreation is considerably more burdensome. A man needs a woman to have children and, since the sexual act happens at a considerable time distance from the birth, they must trust the woman to know that the child is theirs. Controlling women's sexual behaviour has been a primary way for men to ensure they support their own offspring and not those of another man. Stigmatizing illegitimate and unrecognized children has also been a way of maintaining patrilineal patterns of inheritance. Historically, and still in many communities today, a lack of paternal support makes bringing up a child difficult. I note at this point that there are family patterns that do not conform to heterosexual assumptions. Trans men can become pregnant, have babies or choose to abort. Gay and lesbian couples have children and make complex parental decisions. Women choose to have children on their own. I am, however, in this book using language that is gendered because of the longstanding assumptions about women's sexuality, their capacity to reason or not and the presumption of their maternal instinct. Underlying assumptions about women impact on how abortion is talked about; using gender neutral terms for parenting can mask those assumptions.

In this book, I am addressing how we talk about abortion within Christianity, particularly from a pastoral perspective. This means that the ambivalent, and often hostile, attitude to sexual desire that is part of the Western Christian tradition needs to be explored. This theology of sex has been written by men, often celibate men. Women have been depicted at different times as temptresses or as weak creatures in need of protection, either way seen as more open to sin and less able to make rational choices. The Christian valorizing of sexual continence has meant that sexual misconduct has been understood as sinful. Women's virginity has a special place in the stories of saints and most especially in the person of Mary, mother of the Christ-child. She alone was able to hold together the purity of virginity with the role of a mother, portraying the ultimate woman as both chaste and maternal. This chapter will provide a brief reflection on the history of attitudes to sex within the Western Church tradition before looking at some more recent Christian responses to women's sexuality.

## Reproduction and sexed difference

For a new human being to be born, a male sperm and a female egg need to come together. Until recent fertility techniques were perfected, this could only happen through heterosexual sex, in which an erect penis ejaculated into the vagina of an ovulating woman. The man needs to be aroused to have an erection and the orgasmic ejaculation that releases the sperm. The woman may be aroused but this is not necessary; in fact, even her consent is not necessary for conception to happen. Many children are conceived through joyful, loving sex and welcomed into the world. Yet, from the basic facts of reproduction, we note the inequality. Male pleasure is part of the act, and female pleasure, though a possibility, is not a necessity. If conception happens, then the responsibility for bringing this life to birth falls on the woman. She gestates the new life; it is entirely dependent on her body for all it needs. It changes her, limits her, even puts her life in danger. Over nine months, her body becomes increasingly accommodated to the needs of the growing life until the point that she labours a baby into the world. All of this is physically, emotionally and socially costly, and the burden cannot be shared. The human baby is born as a deeply dependent being who will need intense care for many years. A woman's body is able to feed the infant, and women are expected to care lovingly for the child they have borne. Women's bodily capacity to bear and feed children means they have been seen as naturally primed to love and care for them.

The burden for women in the reproductive process is obvious. The issue for men is twofold. They are dependent on a woman if they wish to have offspring; yet, they must trust that woman. Not all children are equally valued. A woman knows the child born of her body; a man wants to know that his sperm enabled this child to be born. If he is to invest in caring for the child, he wants this to be his offspring. This has been and continues to be an important issue in terms of inheritance, preserving the family, the tribe and the nation. In patrilineal societies, where the inheritance of name and property comes through the father, controlling women's sexual behaviour is a way of protecting male lineage. We see this in the biblical texts where the children of Israel can trace their descendants back to their father Abraham. Adultery, sex with someone other than their husband, on the part of women is a serious sin, potentially muddling the bloodline. For much of history and still in many parts of society today, a 'fatherless' child, that is one without a father's acknowledgement, is stigmatized as a problem. The mother of such a child may struggle with little support or resource to care for the child and with social judgement of her and the child's moral standing. Historically, illegitimate sons were barred from many professions. Not all children are equally welcome.

The conceiving of children is not and has never been an exact science. Some sexual couplings result in conception, and some do not. Even now when there is a better understanding of ovulation and fertility, conceiving is still unpredictable. Women who want to be pregnant can find that, despite frequent sex, the longed-for pregnancy does not happen. We note the biblical stories of such women: Sarah, Rachel, Hannah and Elizabeth. Other women conceive even when they hope not to. Once conception has happened, many fertilized eggs simply do not implant in the womb; we still only know some of the reasons for this. Early pregnancy is precarious, and it is estimated that spontaneous miscarriages occur in one in five pregnancies. Pregnancy itself raises potential health problems for the woman and childbirth is physically risky. Women still die of pregnancy complications and in childbirth, even in medically advanced healthcare systems.[2] In the past, before advances in modern medicine, such deaths were far more likely. Medical advancement has also altered the rate of infant mortality. Until the mid-nineteenth century, roughly 50% of infants would die.[3] Reproduction and the early years of life have always been precarious.

Marriage has been the predominant legal relationship that guarantees legitimacy to children and support for a woman in caring for her offspring. In Christian countries, this has been both a civil and a religious commitment, though the role each played has varied. Differences in social status have impacted on how marriages were contracted. Faithfulness in the marriage relationship has traditionally been expected of women, though not always of men. Within marriage, both parties have generally wanted enough children to ensure their future – children who will care for their parents when they are old; children who will carry on the family name. The latter, of course, means that often male children have been preferred to female. Again, not all children are equally welcome. Women who were not married have mainly tried to avoid having children, not least because of the stigma and lack of support for illegitimate children and their mothers. Unmarried women were, and in many cultures are, encouraged to avoid sex prior to marriage, or at least until there was a promise of marriage. Women who were kept as mistresses might have children, recognized and possibly supported, but not legitimate. Women who were prostitutes or simply engaging in any form of unsanctioned relationship would need to find ways to care for any children they had without male support. Women who were raped or seduced might have to bear unacknowledged children with many assumptions about the mother's loose morality. Women who faced the risks of unwanted pregnancy were the most likely to use potions and practices that aimed to prevent pregnancy or end an unwanted one. These historic attempts at abortion will be discussed further in the next chapter.

Women have been judged wanting for not producing children: barren women. They have been blamed for producing the wrong sex of child, especially where inheritance depended on a boy. They have been stigmatized for producing children outside the respectability of marriage: bastard children. Women have been blamed for birthing children with disabilities. They have also been condemned and criminalized for seeking to end an unplanned pregnancy. They have caused themselves serious damage and even died from attempts to abort an unwanted pregnancy. In different parts of the world, women's reproductive lives are still impacted by all of these attitudes. Men can, and do, walk away. They may not know, and they may not care, whether a sexual encounter has led to a pregnancy. None of this is particular to religious attitudes; however, religious ideas about both women and sex have underpinned such judgements. Christianity grew out of the Jewish faith with its scriptural story of a family that became a nation. The stories of the Patriarchs include accounts of infertility that end with the birth of a long-promised son. God is the one who makes the barren woman fruitful, and children are repeatedly described as God's blessing. The Genesis mandate to be fruitful and multiply is taken as a command for humans to procreate.

As daughters of Eve, women are both part of God's good creation made in the image of God and yet also seen as the easily tempted. The account in Genesis 2 that depicts Eve's creation after and out of Adam, followed by her decision to trust the serpent and eat the forbidden fruit, has been traditionally read as marking her need of male oversight. Women pass from their father's house to their husband's, and hope to bear sons who will care for them in the future. The punishment of Eve as recounted in Genesis 3 is to be ruled by her husband, who she desires, and to painfully bear his children: 'I will greatly increase your pangs in childbearing; in pain you shall bring forth children, yet your desire shall be for your husband, and he shall rule over you' (Gen. 3.16). This verse was used to argue against developing pain relief for labouring women. The first letter of Timothy states that women 'will be saved through childbearing' (1 Tim. 2.15). There has been much debate over what this means, but it has traditionally affirmed the understanding that bearing children is women's primary purpose.

The concern that women were more prone to sexual misconduct was present in medical ideas about women's bodies within the Greco-Roman world in which Christianity developed. While male bodies were considered dry and hot, women's bodies were moist, cold and leaky. The regular loss of blood through menstruation meant that women were desirous of sex with men to receive the heated liquid. Women benefited from receiving this male seed as it replenished lost fluid, could help keep the womb in place and, of course, lead to pregnancy. The notion of women's wombs wandering about the body in search of moisture was widely held.[4] Women's need of sex meant that they were often characterized as oversexed and lacking in self-control. The cool dampness of women was necessary for the process of gestation, and many medics assumed that their pleasure in sex was a positive aspect in conception. Men, on the other hand, needed to practise moderation. Excessive sex with its loss of fluid could weaken a man. Self-control was considered a key virtue for men but something that women lacked.[5]

We find a similar understanding of women's sexual desire in the Hebrew Scriptures, both in the positive depiction in the Song of Songs and in the more disturbing imagery of the unfaithful wife who plays the harlot, for instance in the book of Hosea. The image of the unfaithful wife is used in prophetic literature as a metaphor for the lack of faithfulness of the people of Israel towards God. 'What is noticeable about the prophetic literature even in its earliest surviving phase is the emphatic connection it makes between sexual misconduct, more than often on the part of women, and infidelity to the God of Israel.'[6] MacCulloch notes that the Greek translation of the Jewish Scriptures, the Septuagint, uses the word *'porneia'* – prostitution – in a particularly spiritualized way. In the context of Scripture, it comes to include 'both fornication and adultery, because they constituted acts of prostitution which were rebellions against God'.[7] So, the connection between sexual misconduct and rebellion against God is present in early Christian morality and shapes a particular view of women. Sexual continence was to be practised before marriage and when widowed. Within the boundaries of marriage, sexual relations are seen as pleasurable for men and women, and, of course, they are meant to be fruitful in producing children. Yet, as the Christian Church develops, the attitude to sex even within marriage becomes more problematic.

## The valorizing of celibacy and virginity

Jesus was unusual for a Jewish rabbi in being unmarried. He had fathered no children, and some of his recorded sayings challenged the primacy of family ties. In Matthew's Gospel, Jesus comments on eunuchs, stating that some 'have made themselves eunuchs for the kingdom of heaven' (Matt. 19.12). Paul, in his first letter to the Corinthians, implies that he is unmarried and that it would be better if Christians who are unmarried could follow his example. Yet, he states that those who are 'burning' with sexual desire would do best to marry (1 Cor. 7.9). Most commentators suggest that Paul writes in the belief that Christ will soon return and the faithful need to be ready to focus on the ensuing kingdom rather than building up their family. Jesus and Paul were understood to be focusing on the things of God, not the concerns of family life and inheritance. However, Paul was supportive of marriage and sex, suggesting that husband and wife should not abstain from sex except by mutual consent for short periods (1 Cor. 7.5). The later epistles, which include household codes, assume that marriage will be the normal relationship. Sexual continence was considered appropriate outside of marriage, but this was likely to be for a limited period before marriage or during widowhood.

However, this sense of becoming a 'eunuch' for the sake of the kingdom and following Paul's example of a 'better way' came to be interpreted as a call for a life of permanent sexual renunciation. Such a life was considered a witness to faith and offered a path to a deeper spiritual life. Origen of Alexandria, the influential third-century theologian, is said to have castrated himself, literally making himself a eunuch for the kingdom. That such practices were later forbidden by the Church shows that some believed them to be legitimate spiritual practices. Interestingly, this call to sexual chastity was followed by women as well as men. The early church communities brought together people of different backgrounds. Men and women worshipped together, and all passed through the same ritual of baptism. There is evidence that women were involved in ministry and leadership. The Acts of the Apostles notes that many women, as well as men, were imprisoned as part of Saul's persecution of Christians. Waves of persecution would follow over the first centuries. The stories of those who were tortured and martyred were told as examples of heroic faithfulness to strengthen and inspire their fellow Christians who might themselves face persecution. The courage of female martyrs was considered remarkable because of the presumed weakness of women. That even weak women could be sustained by the strengthening presence of Christ to keep the faith, despite horrendous torture, was a witness to the power of Christianity.

The stories of martyrs offered a particular understanding of heroic faithfulness, modelling self-control in the face of torture and threat. Where martyrdom was not a threat, then showing bodily self-control over sexual desires became a heroic sign of trust in God. Both martyrdom and sexual continence bear witness to the power of Christ to transform lives and enable individuals to overcome bodily weakness for the sake of spiritual gains. Among the inspirational tales of faith and martyrdom that circulated in the second century was an apocryphal book The Acts of Paul, which contained the story of Thecla, a young woman who is converted by Paul's preaching. She leaves her fiancé and then endures terrible persecutions as she defies her family, refuses marriage and follows Paul's Christian teaching. Central to Thecla's story of heroic Christian faith was her virginity, and her cult grew rapidly. She appealed to women and to men, and Brown notes that this 'particular form of sexual renunciation – the preservation of a virgin state in the strict sense ... increasingly caught the imagination of all Christians'.[8]

Whereas virginity and sexual continence had been appropriate before betrothal and marriage, early Christianity offered the possibility of a permanent celibate lifestyle dedicated to Christ. Young women became consecrated virgins for the sake of Christ. Young men wrestled with the temptations of the flesh as they committed themselves to permanent sexual continence.

Widows refrained from remarrying and embraced celibacy. Brown writes: 'By the year 300, Christian asceticism, invariably associated with some form or other of perpetual sexual renunciation, was a well-established feature of most regions of the Christian world.'[9] The capacity to control sexual desire, and the valorizing of those who could do so, has left a long shadow on Christian ideas about sex and sexuality. The temptations of the flesh became associated with the devil's attempt to lead Christians from the true path. For men, women were often the source of temptation and unwanted sexual urges, and so women could be seen as the devil's tool; after all, they are the daughters of Eve.

Where did this leave marriage and the importance of procreation? In Genesis, God had commanded the humans, male and female, to go forth and multiply. If children were a blessing from God, then sexual intercourse was clearly necessary. Was it also godly? Theologians questioned whether Adam and Eve would have had sexual intercourse if they had not been banished from Eden. Origen stated that 'Adam had a body in Paradise; but in Paradise he did not know Eve'.[10] Yet, outside Eden, they did know each other and produced children. Other theologians, such as Augustine, believed that sexual reproduction was part of the ideal human state, but it would have been without lust. Clearly sex was necessary, but it was also problematic. For those who could not practise the continence of the celibate, trying to minimize the overwhelming nature of sexual desire and the pleasure in sexual acts was advised. Marital sex should be undertaken as a conscious act, in the service of God, not for pleasure but for the purpose of procreation. Couples were encouraged to practise restraint in their sexual relationships, abstaining during designated fast days and seasons such as Lent. In a marriage manual, Clement of Alexandria suggested that couples should aim for seemly sex in which they could 'produce children by a reverent, disciplined act of will'.[11] God, it was concluded, offered two ways of life: the one 'above nature', a life of sexual continence, and the other, the 'humble human life' of pure nuptials that produced children.[12] In neither life was sex considered a pleasure to be enjoyed, and any sexual activity other than heterosexual procreative sex was sinful. As MacCulloch writes:

> By the fourth and fifth centuries CE, celibacy, virginity and the ascetic life had won a privileged position over against marriage in the theology and devotional practice of Christian churches. The general message was that it was simply easier to obtain salvation as a celibate than as a sexually active married person.[13]

From the third century onwards, a way of reading the parable of the sower expressed the hierarchy of lifestyle. The parable found in the synoptic Gospels ends with the seed in the good soil yielding fruit, 'thirty, sixty and a hundredfold' (Matt. 13.1–23). The yield of a hundredfold was equated with martyrs, sixtyfold for virgin ascetics and thirtyfold for the married. MacCulloch comments: 'The general consensus, right into the medieval period, was to divide the differential yields up between virgins, widows and the married, to the distinct disadvantage of the married, down at the thirtyfold mark.'[14] The higher value of celibacy led towards a celibate priesthood, though it would take time for this to become universal. Bishop Ambrose in the late fourth century was a strong advocate of clergy celibacy. Mary's virginity was central to his understanding of the Incarnation and his attitude to sex. Christ, he argued, had been conceived without sexual intercourse and without any expression of sexual desire. Christ's body was unscarred by the taint of sexual origin and was, he maintained, free from sexual impulses. It was not possible for any other human to be conceived without sex, but they could live in a way that mastered their sexual desires. Those who handled the body of Christ in the Eucharist should be free from sexual taint. Mary's virginal body became a site for veneration, and the beginnings of the doctrine of her permanent virginity were developed.

## Augustine on sex and original sin

Ambrose was to have a profound influence on Augustine of Hippo. Augustine was sexually experienced; before his conversion to Christianity, he had lived with a concubine, with whom he had a child. That relationship ended because he was betrothed to marry a woman considered his social equal, though not yet old enough. Having become a Christian, studying with Ambrose, Augustine decided to forgo his marriage and accept permanent celibacy when he was ordained. He became a Bishop in 395, and his extensive theological writing has shaped Western Christianity. In his writings, he returns at different points to the question of sexual intercourse and the problem of male sexual desire. He is particularly concerned about the lack of control men have over their sexual organs and the loss of control at ejaculation. He writes 'so intense is the pleasure that when it reaches its climax there is an almost total extinction of mental alertness; the intellectual sentries, as it were, are overwhelmed.'[15] This inability for the will to control the body Augustine connects to human sinfulness. Reflecting on Genesis, he concludes that Adam and Eve, as fully human beings, would have had sexual intercourse to conceive children in Paradise. Yet, before the Fall, they would have been able to do so fully aligning their rational will to the act, so without any lust or loss of control. After the Fall, the result of Adam and Eve's disobedience, human beings cannot fully control their own will, and the sexual act is a clear example of this. When Eve and Adam ate the forbidden fruit, they surrendered to temptation, to self-gratification; rather than obedience to God, this is concupiscence. The inability to ejaculate without an overwhelming moment of gratification shows that a fatal deposit of concupiscence is present in sexual intercourse, left by the Fall.[16] As all are born through a sexual act, so all inherit this original sin. Only Christ, born of a pure virgin, who had 'no eddy of uncontrolled feeling' at the moment of conception, is human without the sinful consequence of the Fall. This connection of sexual desire and sexual pleasure – even if unwilled

– to human sinfulness has had a lasting impact on the Christian attitude towards sexual sin.

Augustine also connected sex to shame. 'For why is the especial work of parents withdrawn and hidden even from the eyes of their children, except that it is impossible for them to be occupied in laudable procreation without shameful lust?' Margaret Kamitsuka writes: 'Shame was the existential proof for Augustine's somewhat tortured conscience that sexual pleasure – even within the bounds of marriage – was in fact sinful.'[17] Marriage mattered, and Augustine could recommend it as a form of friendship, yet the sex within marriage was meant to be careful, controlled, engaged in stoically for the purpose of procreation alone. Augustine's thoughts on the link between sexual intercourse and original sin meant that there was no room for a theology of sexual pleasure, even within marriage. Sexual continence was a sign of spiritual strength, a mark of holiness for men and women. The only justification for sexual intercourse was procreation. Any sexual activity for pleasure was a form of self-gratification and was thus sinful. As MacCulloch writes, 'The Western Church was thus launched on an inescapable association between shame and sex, not excluding marital sexuality.'[18]

Theology was mostly written by bishops and monks, celibate men who increasingly kept their distance from women. Women saints were praised for their virginity, and the greatest of all the saints was Mary, who was both pure virgin and mother. Women who married faced multiple pregnancies, the risks of childbirth and the grief of high infant mortality. The medieval book of Marjorie Kempe recounts her frequent requests for her husband to agree to sexual abstinence. She had 14 children, a severe psychotic episode after her first childbirth and a desperate longing to be free to make pilgrimages and focus on her faith.[19] He was not so keen on abstinence. That men engaged in sex outside the marriage relationship was recognized in the acceptance of prostitution and brothels. Augustine observed that 'if you remove harlots from society, you will disrupt everything because of lust'. By the thirteenth century, this had morphed into a phrase attributed to Aquinas, 'remove the sewer, and you fill the place with a stench ... take away whores from the world, and you will fill it with sodomy.'[20] MacCulloch notes that prostitution was deemed non-reproductive sex (one wonders how the women engaged in such sex ensured that it was or managed when it was not). Such women could be saved, and found an unlikely saint in Mary Magdalene, who, due to a well disseminated sermon by Gregory IX, was identified as the sinful woman in Luke 7. 'Magdalene houses' to redeem 'fallen' women became an aspect of the Church's ministry even into the twentieth century.

## The Reformation

The Reformation challenged clerical celibacy and the suggestion that celibacy was the superior Christian way of life. Requiring celibacy was seen as contrary to both God's word and to nature. Luther wrote: 'To spurn marriage is to act against God's calling ... and against nature's urging.'[21] After his marriage to the ex-nun Katharine, he wrote warmly of marital love, including sexual intimacy. Calvin also wrote positively about the marriage relationship. For both, marriage was a protection from sexual sin and promiscuity. Within marriage, sexual intimacy was good. Children were a blessing, but the sexual act was not tethered to the intention of procreation; sexual intimacy strengthened the marriage relationship. This view was grounded in a reading of Genesis 2 as constituting marriage prior to the Fall. Adam and Eve were understood to reveal the natural ordering of men and women in a married relationship. Thus, Protestantism moved away from the privileging of celibacy and sexual renunciation as 'the superior' way of living.

Marriage was understood to be God's design for humankind, and having children was part of that – not simply having them, but bringing them up as godly people. A stable marriage relationship was important for this, and sexual intimacy both produced children and strengthened the marriage. Sex outside of marriage threatened the good estate of marriage, an argument that continues into modern debates about sexuality. Current discussions about same-sex relationships and whether they can be blessed or recognized as marriages draw on theologies of marriage that prioritize heterosexual, procreative sex as God's design. Those within the Church of England arguing for a recognition of same-sex committed relationships as worthy of blessing are accused of trying to change the traditional doctrine of marriage. This Reformation understanding of marriage is set out in the Church of England's Book of Common Prayer; the first edition published in 1549, revised in 1662, outlined the purpose of marriage.

> First, It was ordained for the procreation of children, to be brought up in the fear and nurture of the Lord, and to the praise of his holy Name.
> Secondly, It was ordained for a remedy against sin, and to avoid fornication; that such persons as have not the gift of continency might marry, and keep themselves undefiled members of Christ's body.
> Thirdly, It was ordained for the mutual society, help, and comfort, that the one ought to have of the other, both in prosperity and adversity.

It is clear that procreation is the primary reason for marriage and that marriage is also meant to provide a moral place for sexual behaviour for those not gifted with continence.

Sexual activity outside of the marital relationship was deemed sinful. John Witte writes: 'Protestants also recognized traditional sex crimes like adultery, concubinage, prostitution, incest, polygamy, sodomy, abortion, infanticide, and child abuse as violations of natural and biblical morality.'[22] He notes the moral codes established in Calvinism designed to curb inappropriate sexual expression, even dancing.[23] Public punishment of sexual misdemeanours was a normal aspect of Protestant society. MacCulloch writes, 'in 1600, it would have been widely accepted that such matters as fornication and adultery should be punished publicly and exemplarily by corporeal punishment.'[24] Yet by the end of the eighteenth century, such public punishments were no longer happening, and sexual morality had become a private rather than a public matter. In 1787, the Church courts in Britain lost their right to prosecute people for premarital fornication.

By the late eighteenth century, developments in understanding the human body in terms of medicine and reproduction changed the traditionally held views of male and female bodies. Sexual difference was highlighted not just in bodily terms but also in sexed virtues and characteristics. Women were no longer governed by their wandering womb and excess fluidity, which meant they were also not conceived of as being sexually voracious. Instead, women's natural purity and modesty were stressed. Mary Wollstonecraft, in her essay *The Vindication of the Rights of Women* published in 1792, critiqued these sexed virtues, saying that they denied women the right to be educated and to use their own rationality. It would take time for women's education to become mainstream in the twentieth century and for modern feminism to challenge the gender assumptions about women's irrationality and passivity. It is interesting to note that theology was one of the last areas of academic study opened to women. It was popularly feared that too much education for women might lead to a neglect of marriage and childbearing.

By the beginning of the twentieth century, education was being opened to women. Women were campaigning for access to training, professional jobs and the right to vote. They were even campaigning for the right to ordination. The language of the marriage service was found to be a little strong, and the proposed 1928 Prayer Book in the Church of England removed terms such as 'fornication' and 'sin'. So, the second reason for marriage became: 'It was ordained in order that the natural instincts and affections, implanted by God, should be hallowed and directed aright ...' This suggested wording offers a more positive view of the naturalness of sexual instincts, link-ing them to affection and as God given. Procreation is still the first purpose. By 2000, when the current Church of England marriage service was licensed, having children has become the third reason for marriage: the first is companionship, and the second speaks of 'the delight and tenderness of sexual union'. This service recognizes that children may have already been born before the marriage and even that a couple may wish to marry intending to be childless. The sense that the purpose of sex is mainly procreative has been muted.

In *Something to Celebrate: Valuing Families in Church and the Society*, published in 1995, the Church of England made the headlines for suggesting that the term 'living in sin' to refer to cohabiting couples should no longer be used. It wanted to recognize different family patterns and to remove the notion of sin where couples were not married. While attitudes to cohabitation have changed markedly in modern British society, the official Church of England position is that sex outside of marriage falls short of God's ideal. The Bishop of Dover shocked General Synod in a debate on same-sex relations in July 2024 when she challenged the suggestion that sex outside marriage was sinful.

> All our children and grandchildren are having sex, and yet I do not hear us saying 'We're not going to walk with them' ... more than half the people who come to us for marriage are living together and they're having sex. So, what is it about homosexual [sex that] we're reacting in such a visceral way?[25]

She is certainly right that while official Church teaching continues to maintain that sex outside of marriage is not ideal, or even sinful, few couples offer different addresses when booking weddings, and few churches would quibble about the marital status of a couple bringing a child for baptism. Both attitudes have altered since the early days of my ministry in the late twentieth century.

However, the shifts in accepting sexual activity outside marriage have been more pragmatic than theological. Social attitudes have changed as sexual gratification is portrayed as a positive aspect of life for men and women. The development of relatively reliable contraception from the latter part of the twentieth century has, for the most part, separated the idea of sex from procreation. Where safe legal abortion exists, it can offer a backstop to failed contraception. The stigma of being born outside marriage has significantly reduced, meaning that having a child, even as a single mother, is more socially acceptable. Marriage happens at different points in relationships, sometimes after children and mostly after a period of cohabitation. People plan when to have children, although that does not always mean they come as planned. The impact of contraception on these changes will be explored further in the next chapter.

Yet, the sexual revolution has not necessarily brought women equality in sexual relationships. The #MeToo movement brought to public attention the high levels of sexual harassment and assault that many women encounter. Studies of university campuses in the US, Canada and UK show a worrying normalization of male dominance and female passivity that has been described by some researchers as 'rape culture'. McCabe, commenting on US campus culture, suggests that 'desirability is the expected role for women to play in order to participate in the social culture'.[26] The need to be seen as desirable can make women reluctant to acknowledge, even to themselves, the abusive nature of some of the sexual encounters they experience. The widespread use of pornography reinforces the idea of women's availability for male sexual gratification. She concludes that 'the gender roles available to both men and women limit the possibility of a full personhood and a well-rounded sexuality for all'.[27] Questions of what constitutes consent in sexual encounters is problematic as will be discussed further in Chapter 3. This sense of sex as principally about recreation and gratification, is a far cry from sex as principally for procreation. Writing from a Roman Catholic perspective, McCabe highlights how a sexual ethics that focus on whether sex is procreative or not is inadequate to address the lived experience of today's society. She quotes Andolsen: 'The fundamental evil in a revised code of Roman Catholic Sexual ethics should not be nonprocreative sexual activity: rather it should be coercive sexual activity.'[28]

## Talking about sex and women

Over the latter half of the twentieth century and into the twenty-first century, Churches have needed to navigate changing social attitudes to the role of women and sexual behaviour. The theological debates have focused on access to church leadership roles and the defence of marriage. Many Churches have welcomed women into leadership and explored theologies that affirm the common humanity of men and women, and the differing gifts found across the sexes. Where there has been a desire to limit women's access to areas of church leadership, an essential God-given difference between men and women is stressed. This inevitably links women to motherhood. John Paul II, writing to women in 1988 in *Mulieres Dignitatum*, affirms their maternal nature, which can be fulfilled through actual motherhood or through spiritual motherhood. Pope Francis refers to 'the special concern which women show to others, which finds a particular, even if not exclusive, expression in motherhood'.[29]

The rise of complementarian theology in conservative evangelical Churches stresses the role of women as the ones who bear and bring up children. Young women have a duty to stay pure until they meet the right man and can then fulfil the role of supportive wife and loving mother. There is an expectation that women play an important role in minimizing the temptations of premarital sex, by not leading boys on. Young men will also be taught to control their sexual desires. The theological ethicist Stanley Hauerwas, who is strongly opposed to abortion, does emphasize the need to address male behaviour. 'As far as today's Church is concerned, we must start condemning male promiscuity.' Yet, he also seems to imply that women need to be the ones to say no. The answer is to stress the prohibition of sex outside marriage. 'One of the good things about the church's understanding of marriage is that it helps us to get a handle on making men take responsibility for their progeny.'[30] It is notable that sex is still being understood as primarily procreative.

Churches have found themselves defending the institution of marriage for two reasons: first, the rise in divorce and the question of remarriage; second, as lesbian, gay and bisexual couples have campaigned for equal marriage. *Issues in Human Sexuality*, published by the Church of England in 1991, speaks positively of heterosexual sexual desire and pleasure. The level of bodily intimacy between a couple, it maintains, needs to be matched by fidelity and commitment. So, sex belongs within the commitment of marriage. Having stressed sexual intimacy as something that sustains the relationship, there is a need to revert to the issue of procreation in order to critique committed gay sex, showing that this is not part of God's design for humanity. There is much more that could be said on these issues, but the fixation on how the Church can or cannot recognize LGBTQ relationships has prevented a serious reflection on the wider issues of sexual behaviour. Maintaining that any sexual relationship outside marriage is sinful has provided a neat way for those within the Church to prohibit gay and lesbian relationships without appearing to discriminate. Conservative evangelicals continue to stress sexual continence before marriage and to oppose any kind of committed sexual relationship between same-sex couples. The charity Living Out supports those who are sexually attracted to the same sex to embrace permanent sexual continence throughout their life as a witness to their faith, in language that echoes early Church valorization of celibacy.

As ideas about marriage change, as women's careers are taken seriously and as the decision to have children becomes for many a considered position, the period of life in which procreation is the focus of any sexual relationship has become much smaller. The morality of consensual sex outside marriage, particularly in the years before or after a marriage, needs to be addressed by Christian ethics. As noted in this chapter, the history of such ethics has rarely considered women's sexual desires. Former Archbishop of Canterbury Rowan Williams suggests that we might reflect on the capacity for joy in sex.

> It puts the question which is also raised for some kinds of moralist by the existence of the clitoris in women; something whose function is joy. If the creator were quite so instrumentalist in 'his' attitude to sexuality, these hints of prodigality and redundancy in the way the whole thing works might cause us to worry about whether he was, after all, in full control of it. But if God made us for joy ...?[31]

There needs to be a theology that recognizes women's pleasure, which is not necessary for conception but should be part of a respectful sexual encounter. Teaching material prepared for Church of England schools presents the importance of negotiated, mutually gratifying sex within a committed relationship.[32] A wider discussion of these ideas could help challenge the historic Christian connection between sexual pleasure, shame and sin. Taking women seriously and equipping them to be confident in articulating their sexual desires needs to go alongside teaching boys and men to value and respect women. Where couples can talk about their sexual relationship, valuing mutuality, they are more likely to make good use of contraception and minimize the risks of unplanned pregnancy. Recognizing changing social patterns of life means that the idea of 'commitment' may be used in place of marriage as a way of critiquing sex in uncommitted, casual and coercive encounters and prioritizing the importance of consent.

## How do we talk about abortion?

Embedded theological ideas can impact our opinions, even at a subliminal level. The long history of Christianity associating sex with sin and shame can colour opinions about abortion.

The presumption that abortion decisions are mainly made by the sexually transgressive and sexually incontinent leads to judging the woman's perceived behaviour. She has definitely had sexual intercourse, and the fact that she does not want to be pregnant means this sex was not aimed at procreation. The assumption may be that she does not want the child because it is the result of an illegitimate relationship – even though that is not necessarily the case. It may be deemed that, by having sex in the first place, she should face the consequences of her actions and that means having a baby. It is important to remember that the consequences for a woman are far more burdensome and life-changing than for the man. If this is a case of premarital sex, then there may be encouragement for a wedding before the child is born, or soon after. Wider society has, as noted above, become less concerned about children born out of wedlock, but some Christian communities still find it problematic.

Alongside the history of a negative attitude to sexual pleasure, Christianity has an ambiguous attitude to the place and purpose of women. Women may be temptresses, 'leading the man on'. Or they may be morally weaker, easily led astray. Either way, the Church has traditionally seen the role of mother as the primary vocation of women and, to some extent, the saving role. To reject motherhood can thus be considered a turning against women's intended nature and a form of disobedience to God's plan. If children are seen as a gift of God, then to reject this gift is perceived as rejecting God's giving. In Chapter 3, the issues around unintended pregnancy and God's providence will be further explored. The purpose of setting out this brief history of the Christian tradition's ambiguity about both sex and women is to encourage a questioning of the embedded theology that each of us brings to the question of abortion.

It is possible to both be concerned about sexual hedonism and casual sex while also critiquing the historic association of sexual pleasure with shame and even sin. There is much that is not healthy about modern attitudes to sex, and women are statistically more likely to be on the receiving end of abusive, even violent, sexual behaviour. Churches need to critique sexual violence, exploitation and the commodification of sex. They also need to have better conversations about the place of sexual pleasure in human lives. Encouraging the values of respect, commitment, mutual pleasure and responsibility is necessary. Giving young people the language to talk to each other about sex is important: sex education that teaches both how to wait until you feel ready and how to use contraception is shown to delay the age at which first sexual encounters happen.[33]

Yet too often, the perception and the reality is that Christianity retains its historic view of sex as shameful and potentially sinful. The idea that sex is sinful before marriage and then miraculously good post-marriage is hard for people to understand. In lived experience, what is the difference? Christianity's historic antipathy to homosexuality plays a part in negative attitudes to sexual pleasure and the place of non-procreative sex. Debates about same-sex relationships tend to re-emphasize procreation as the purpose of marital sex and hence marriage as the rightful place for sex. Yet, modern contraception and a wider understanding of sexual behaviour have altered this understanding. A sexual relationship is for pleasure, for strengthening intimacy and only for having children when the timing is deemed appropriate. Of course, 'accidents' happen and many will be embraced, starting a family earlier than planned, having more children than intended, choosing to bring up a child alone. When an 'accident' cannot be embraced, then abortion may be the appropriate response. If the act of having an abortion is proclaimed as sinful, then it will be hard for women to talk to those within the Church about why they have decided that it is the best decision in these circumstances. Chapter 3 will look further at the issues around unintended pregnancy, and Chapter 5 will return to the language of sin.

## HOW DO WE TALK ABOUT ABORTION?

## Notes

1 Ted G. Jelen, 2024, 'Public Opinion and Attitudes toward Abortion: Patterns across Religious Traditions', in *The Oxford Handbook of Religious Perspectives on Reproductive Ethics*, ed. Dena S. Davis, 1st edn, Oxford: Oxford University Press, pp. 459–74, https://doi.org/10.1093/oxfordhb/9780190633202.013.32, accessed 24.04.2025.
2 'Maternal Death Rates in the UK', n.d., https://www.ox.ac.uk/news/2024-01-11-maternal-death-rates-uk-have-increased-levels-not-seen-almost-20-years, accessed 30.04.2025.
3 Saloni Dattani et al., 2023, 'Child and Infant Mortality', https://ourworldindata.org/child-mortality, accessed 30.04.2025.
4 Helen King, 2024, *Immaculate Forms: Uncovering the History of Women's Bodies*, London: Profile Books. See her chapter on the womb.
5 Diarmaid MacCulloch, 2024, *Lower than the Angels: A History of Sex and Christianity*, London: Allen Lane, pp. 49–50.
6 MacCulloch, *Lower than the Angels*, p. 17.
7 MacCulloch, *Lower than the Angels*, p. 55.
8 Peter Brown, 1988, *The Body and Society: Men, Women and Sexual Renunciation in Early Christianity*, Lectures on the History of Religions, N.S., 13, New York: Columbia University Press, p. 159.
9 Brown, *The Body and Society*, p. 202.
10 Brown, *The Body and Society*, p. 175.
11 Margaret D. Kamitsuka, 2014, 'Sexual Pleasure', in Adrian Thatcher, ed., *The Oxford Handbook of Theology, Sexuality, and Gender*, Oxford: Oxford University Press, p. 506.
12 Brown, *The Body and Society*, p. 205.
13 MacCulloch, *Lower than the Angels*, p. 167.
14 MacCulloch, *Lower than the Angels*, p. 123.
15 Augustine (trans. Henry Scowcroft Bettenson), 1981, *Concerning the City of God against the Pagans*, Harmondsworth: Penguin, p. 577.
16 Brown, *The Body and Society*, p. 422.
17 Kamitsuka, 'Sexual Pleasure', p. 507.
18 MacCulloch, *Lower than the Angels*, p. 173.
19 Margery Kempe, 1985, *The Book of Margery Kempe*, Penguin Classics, Harmondsworth, Middlesex: Penguin..
20 MacCulloch, *Lower than the Angels*, p. 306.
21 John Witte, 2014, 'Sex and Marriage in the Protestant Tradition 1500–1900', in Adrian Thatcher, ed., *The Oxford Handbook of Theology, Sexuality, and Gender*, Oxford: Oxford University Press, p. 307.
22 Witte, 'Sex and Marriage', p. 306.
23 Witte, 'Sex and Marriage', p. 310.
24 MacCulloch, *Lower than the Angels*, pp. 373–4.

25 Francis Martin and Tim Wyatt, 2023, 'General Synod digest: Update on same-sex blessings underwhelms members', *Church Times*, 14 July, https://www.churchtimes.co.uk/articles/2023/14-july/news/uk/general-synod-digest-update-on-same-sex-blessings-underwhelms-members, accessed 30.04.2025.

26 Megan K. McCabe, 2018, 'A Feminist Catholic Response to the Social Sin of Rape Culture', *Journal of Religious Ethics* 46(4), p. 640, https://doi.org/10.1111/jore.12239, accessed 30.04.2025.

27 McCabe, 'A Feminist Catholic Response', p. 644.

28 McCabe, 'A Feminist Catholic Response', p. 645.

29 Vatican Press, 2013, 'Apostolic Exhortation *Evangelii Gaudium* of the Holy Father Francis', https://www.vatican.va/content/francesco/en/apost_exhortations/documents/papa-francesco_esortazione-ap_20131124_evangelii-gaudium.html, accessed 30.04.2025.

30 Stanley Hauerwas, 1991, 'Abortion Theologically Understood', https://jbburnett.com/resources/hauerwas,%20abortion%20theologically%20understood.pdf, accessed 30.04.2025.

31 Quoted in King, *Immaculate Forms*, p. 187.

32 Diocese of Bristol, n.d., *Goodness and Mercy*, RSHE for Church of England Schools, https://goodnessandmercy.co.uk/teaching-resources, accessed 30.04.2025.

33 Laura Duberstein Lindberg and Isaac Maddow-Zimet, 2012, 'Consequences of Sex Education on Teen and Young Adult Sexual Behaviors and Outcomes', *Journal of Adolescent Health* 51(4), October, pp. 332–8, https://www.guttmacher.org/news-release/2012/sex-education-linked-delay-first-sex, accessed 30.04.2025.

2

# Abortion and Contraception: Changing Attitudes

In 2001, at a seminar that brought together key people involved in the passing of the 1967 Abortion Act in the UK, the politician David Steel, the proposer of the bill, commented that the present generation 'are somehow led to believe that abortion was invented in 1966 ... They think that there was a world in which abortion did not take place until this awful Act was passed.'[1] Abortion may be a topical issue, but it is not a modern phenomenon. Throughout history, some women, faced with a pregnancy in circumstances where they felt unable to continue to gestate and birth a child, tried to find ways to end the pregnancy. Abortions happened, and still happen. Certain plants or combinations of plants, poisons and physical interventions were utilized in the past in the hope that a miscarriage could be induced. Sometimes they will have worked, and the knowledge of such procedures would be shared. Medical interventions to save the mother's life by aborting the child have also been documented. Many of the methods to end pregnancy risk harm to the mother as well; even so, women have knowingly taken risks because of their desperation. In the modern world, in countries where abortion is not legal, this does not mean there are no abortions, just more unsafe ones and higher rates of maternal death.

For much of history, the difference between preventing pregnancy and ending an early pregnancy has been less clear than in modern understanding. This meant advice on herbs and potions to prevent pregnancy or restore menstruation might

## ABORTION AND CONTRACEPTION

have covered both contraception and what would now be deemed early abortions. The medical, philosophical and religious understanding of the female body and reproduction was different, with conception being understood as a process rather than a moment. Women have irregular menstrual cycles for many reasons, not least malnutrition. The difference between a late period and an early miscarriage is not easy to distinguish, particularly in the days before accurate pregnancy testing. Infant mortality was high until the late nineteenth century, when it began to fall. Married women were mostly concerned with questions of fertility and the survival of their babies. Preventing pregnancy and aborting an unintended pregnancy was therefore more likely to be a concern of the unmarried and sex workers. The Church, as noted in the previous chapter, championed procreation in marriage and saw all other forms of sex as sinful; thus, contraception and abortion were both sinful as they interfere with the procreative property of sex. Yet, early interventions did not carry the same weight as interventions later in pregnancy because of ideas about the human soul. As noted already, sex for pleasure was self-gratification and as such was sinful; even marital sexual pleasure was considered problematic.

During the twentieth century, the concept of birth control as 'family planning' changed attitudes to contraception. Falling infant mortality rates meant that without some form of management couples would have more children than they wanted or could care for. Planning the birth of children, or at least preventing the birth of too many, began to be seen as being responsible and prudent. This understanding changed the attitude to contraception in mainline Protestant Churches, led by the Anglican Church, but not that of the Roman Catholic Church. The use of contraception within marriage, and later outside it, meant families could be planned according to the resources of the couple, not simply given by God. Abortion however, remained both illegal (under the Offences Against The Person Act 1861 – see page 34) and sinful. Yet, women continued to utilize 'folklore' and illegal abortion to end unplanned pregnancies, including married women seeking to limit the number of children they had. This chapter will look at the move to decriminalize abortion in the UK. This culminated in the 1967 Abortion Act. The justification for legal abortion was to provide safe abortion procedures, replacing the many unsafe practices that women were resorting to – so-called 'backstreet abortions', which risked serious health consequences or the women's deaths. This concern to stop these has shaped the response of most mainline Protestant Churches. In the UK, the Church of England, the Methodist Church and Church of Scotland all came to accept that abortion might at times be necessary, yet clearly delineated it from contraception defined as family planning. The Church of England's statements had a particular influence on legislation as the Established Church in England. In discussing the changing attitudes to contraception and abortion, it is interesting to note that the former became seen in protestant theology as responsible family planning. Abortion, however, is not usually understood as being an acceptable method of family planning even though many happen after failures in contraception.

In looking at this history from a UK perspective, I note the comments of the American historian Leslie Reagan about differences between the UK and the USA. The campaign for legalized abortion in the UK was driven by women who were mainly shaped by socialist feminism.[2] They were joined by doctors concerned for women's wellbeing. The primary concern was for equal access for all women to safe medical procedures to end a pregnancy. The high numbers of maternal deaths and serious injuries from unsafe practices highlighted inequality. Safe abortions were procurable by those who could afford them, so this loss of life and health was predominantly impacting poorer women. The inability to control family size and the physical, emotional and financial strains of large families were also exacerbated by poverty, lack of education and lack of choices. Where women could not negotiate with their husbands or partners about their sex life, there was little they could do to limit the number of times they conceived.

All of this meant that women's ability to be good mothers to their children was compromised. This concern for women who became pregnant in circumstances where they could not look after a child because they were unmarried or where they had too many children employed ideas about responsible mothering.

Although issues of foetal health impacted attitudes to abortion in the USA, during the 1960s it would be the campaigning of second-wave feminists that eventually enabled legal abortion in the Roe vs Wade judgement of 1973. The overturning of this decision in 2022 has limited access to abortion in many parts of the USA. The campaigns in the 1970s drew on the language of rights and bodily autonomy rather than responsible mothering. 'A woman's right to choose' has remained a recognizable pro-abortion slogan. While important, the rights language has allowed the debate to focus on competing rights of the woman and the developing life. This can too easily be characterized as women being anti-maternal; it also raises issues about whether women in poverty and other kinds of oppression have choices. This last point has been taken up by the Reproductive Justice movement.[3]

As noted in the introduction, abortions happen, and thinking pastorally about them means understanding that this is not a modern phenomenon. The change in twentieth-century attitudes to contraception reinforces the shift from seeing sex as principally procreative explored in the last chapter. The different position of the Roman Catholic Church in retaining the emphasis on procreation is a key element in the opposition to both contraception and abortion. Within protestant theology, the tendency is to see contraception as responsible and abortion as irresponsible. This needs to be examined. If it is recognized that many abortion decisions are decisions about responsible parenting, then the suggestion that these are selfish decisions in which women are putting themselves before this potential child can be challenged. This is important when discussing abortion within Christian contexts where the language of self-sacrifice is often equated with Christian discipleship.

HOW DO WE TALK ABOUT ABORTION?

## Historical views on contraception and abortion

In the first centuries of the Church, ideas about pregnancy were shaped by Greek and Roman medicine. The classicist Helen King writes: 'Since conception was a gradual process taking place over several months, the line between abortion and contraception was also drawn at a point different from our own.'[4] There were varied views on how the sperm – which it was believed contained all or the major components of the new life – developed within the woman into an embryo and then a baby, and what role the woman's body played. However, it was agreed that this life needed to be formed in the womb, and this took time. For Christian theologians, there was also the question of when the soul united with the body; it was generally believed that this could not happen until the body had developed into a recognizably human form. Influenced by the work of Aristotle and Galen, male children were considered stronger and thus formed earlier. Female babies developed where a male was not able to form and came together at a later stage. The predominant view of the early Church was that God infused the foetus with a soul when it was formed. From this point, the foetus had the capability of responding to God. Attempting to end a pregnancy before the foetus was formed clearly interfered with the procreative nature of sex and so was wrong but was more akin to trying to prevent the pregnancy than aborting a formed foetus. The former was a lesser offence not least because it would often be difficult to distinguish an early miscarriage from an induced one.

This differentiation between a formed and unformed foetus was justified from Scripture. Exodus 21.22–25 discusses penalties for the harming of a pregnant woman who gets in the way of a fight. The Hebrew speaks of two circumstances: one where her 'children come out' while she is unharmed, which requires the paying of a fine; the other where there is harm to the woman, even death, which would be treated as 'an eye for an eye'. However, the Greek Septuagint translation, that would have been widely used by early Christian theologians,

## ABORTION AND CONTRACEPTION

implies that the difference is not between the loss of the pregnancy and the harm to the woman but between the loss of an unformed or a formed foetus. This translation may have been influenced by the philosophical ideas described above. It was taken as scriptural affirmation of the difference between an unformed and formed foetus; the loss of the unformed was not manslaughter. This understanding justified a lesser penalty for accidental – and, by extension, intentional – aborting of an early pregnancy. This passage is still debated in discussions about abortion and personhood within the womb: does it show a point when abortion is allowed, or even point to a connection between personhood and a stage of pregnancy?[5]

The theological differentiation between formed and unformed was also a practical one. The early months of pregnancy are unstable. Without the benefits of modern pregnancy tests, there was a lack of clarity about whether someone was or was not pregnant, whether a late period or early miscarriage was induced or spontaneous. The generally held notion of when a foetus was formed and ensouled made sense of 'quickening', the point at about four months into pregnancy at which a woman can feel the movement of the baby, and this movement was taken as indicative of a formed foetus. Pregnancy loss prior to quickening was not the loss of an ensouled baby and so no provision was made for treating any remains passed as human remains. Once the foetus was ensouled, then its loss became complicated. It was now a human soul but, tragically, an unbaptized soul and as such not cleansed of original sin. An unbaptized soul was not able to go to heaven. The unbaptized miscarried or stillborn baby could not be buried in consecrated ground. While Augustine, and those who followed his theology of original sin, maintained that such unbaptized infants would not suffer the punishments of hell, neither could they experience the beatific vision of heaven. By 1300, the term 'Limbo' had been developed to talk of this space where the unbaptized infants dwell, not tormented but not fully redeemed. I will return to this issue in the final chapter.

References to abortifacients in ancient lists of herbal and

practical remedies show that there was knowledge of possible ways of ending a pregnancy. However, it is not always clear what the intention of such remedies was. Often described as potentially 'unblocking' menstrual fluid or purging the womb, some historians, notably John Riddle, suggested that all such remedies were references to abortifacients.[6] King suggests a more nuanced reading, maintaining that remedies for purging the womb and restoring menstruation would have been prescribed for a variety of reasons; it is not clear how often this included inducing the miscarriage of an unintended pregnancy.[7] What is clear is that ending pregnancy 'was permitted in all classical cultures, although there was sometimes social disapproval of women whose motive was merely to keep their looks'.[8] She notes that, in the first few centuries, infant mortality was extremely high, so fertility and infant survival were primary concerns for married women, far more so than preventing more children.[9]

Katharine Park makes the same observation about married women in medieval society. However, she writes:

> While the enhancement of fertility greatly concerned married men and women, single women faced the opposite problem: how to terminate pregnancies resulting from illicit sexual liaisons, voluntary or involuntary, which might threaten their employment or damage the honour of their families.[10]

She comments that in the medieval period, 'knowledge regarding abortifacients procedures and preparations – effective or not – circulated widely, and men and women who wished to terminate unwanted pregnancies would have a good idea whom to consult'.[11] As already noted, prostitution was tolerated as a necessity of society, and it is likely that sex workers would have needed access to contraceptive and abortion practices.[12] The term contraception could refer to anything that ended the pregnancy before the foetus was formed. Where women became pregnant outside marriage and went to term, the child born would be illegitimate. The child could be legitimized if she married the father at any point after their birth. Beginning a sexual relationship during betrothal was widely accepted. If the child was not legitimized through marriage, they could be acknowledged and, while remaining a bastard or 'natural' child, would benefit from having a known father. Some could be absorbed into families, but where that was not possible, infants were abandoned, and some even killed at birth or shortly after by their mother. Religious communities and foundling hospitals became places where abandoned babies could be left, but many would struggle to thrive. Openings in the walls of convents or 'foundling' wheels existed in medieval times to allow the anonymity of the one leaving a baby. It is interesting to note the reintroduction in modern times of places to anonymously abandon a baby: 'baby boxes' in police or fire stations are provided for the same reasons.[13]

## Making abortion illegal

Writing about the United States in the eighteenth and early nineteenth century, the historian Leslie Reagan says: 'The common law's attitude towards pregnancy was based on the understanding of pregnancy and human development as a process rather than an absolute moment.'[14] Also that the concept of quickening was still recognized as the point at which ending a pregnancy became a more serious offence. She notes that products to 'restore menstruation', often used to induce an early abortion, were advertised and available through mail order.

The nineteenth century saw legislation both in the USA and the UK that changed the less serious nature of ending a pregnancy before quickening. In the USA, this campaign was led by the American Medical Association, which sought to make ending a pregnancy at any stage illegal. They suggested that quickening was an unreliable and possibly illusory concept, which relied upon the testimony of women. Anti-poison laws passed in the 1820s and 1830s aimed to limit access to poisons commonly taken to induce a miscarriage, and the 1860s–1880s saw laws that removed the importance of quickening, making abortion illegal at any time in pregnancy.[15] In 1873, the Comstock law prevented any 'lewd' material being sent through US post offices and identified products or information about contraception or abortion specifically.

In the UK, though not Scotland, the Offences against the Person Act was passed in 1861 and contained two clauses on abortion. As in the USA, it removed the notion of quickening as the difference between a lesser and more serious offence, which had been present in earlier legislation (1803). It made self-induced miscarriage, or one induced by someone else, punishable with a life sentence, thus making all abortions illegal. The USA laws allowed for therapeutic abortions when doctors felt that it was necessary to preserve the woman's life. This was not made explicit in the UK, but the language of unlawful procedures meant that the concept of a lawful, therapeutic procedure was generally recognized. In the UK, the Infant Life Preservation Act of 1929 specified the crime of killing a child capable of 'being born alive ... before it has an existence independent of its mother'.

These moves to make abortion at any stage of pregnancy illegal did not stop abortions from happening. Reagan recounts the case of undercover reporters in Chicago in 1888 who approached doctors to ask for a termination of an unplanned pregnancy and how their findings shocked readers. Many respectable physicians either made referrals to a doctor who would perform the procedure or offered to perform the procedure themselves. Reagan notes: 'The *Times* investigation made it obvious that physicians were an important source of abortions, and that abortion was part of regular medicine.'[16] It was also clear that many of those seeking abortion were married women, often trying to limit the size of their family. This challenged the perception that all abortions were sought by those who were sexual transgressors. Abortions were happening, but they were illegal and secret. In both the USA and the UK, those with enough money could access the procedure in doctor's offices and clinics where they usually had safe procedures. Those who needed cheaper options continued to utilize poisons, self-inflicted injuries or procedures carried out in non-clinical settings. Complications from poison, infections and poorly managed abortions could be, and often were, fatal. Legislating to prevent abortion did not stop abortions in the past and does not stop them in the present. It may deter some women from seeking an abortion, or make it impossible for them to end the pregnancy, but for many it means accessing illegal abortions, risking serious complications and possible death. It may also lead to a rise in infant mortality.

## Changing attitudes to contraception

Another way of trying to reduce abortions is to prevent pregnancy, and the twentieth century saw an increasing interest in birth control. Those promoting contraceptive products wanted to clearly differentiate between contraception and abortion. The drivers for birth control were a desire to reduce the size of families and in doing so, limit the risks to women of multiple childbirths and possible fatality. They also wanted to reduce the problem of childhood poverty. Some of these campaigners were driven by fears of population growth and by eugenics. The Christian advice for limiting family size, whether Catholic or Protestant, was to advocate sexual abstinence. Since procreation was God's purpose for marital sex, children should be accepted as God's blessing and faith placed in God's provision.

The historian, Simon Szreter, maintains that 'attempted abstinence' was widely used in Britain in the late nineteenth and early twentieth century as a way of limiting family size, though not necessarily for religious reasons. He shows that avoiding sexual intercourse before marriage, marrying later and then reducing the frequency of sex in marriage were all ways to limit pregnancies. The latter could help in reducing family size.[17] These practices contributed to the falling birth rates in England. He maintains that available forms of contraception were not widely known or utilized and were mostly associated with prostitution. Venereal disease was a serious concern for those using prostitutes, and condoms were originally developed to prevent catching sexually transmitted diseases. He writes, 'the prevention of births in general was associated with the most un-Christian activities of prostitutes and fallen women; abortion and infanticide.'[18]

Abortion was resorted to when attempts to avoid pregnancy failed, particularly in those cases where the relationship was irregular. Many of the remedies offered were ineffectual or harmful. For those who continued a pregnancy, the risk of death in childbirth or early infant mortality was considerably higher for unmarried mothers who may not have had a safe place to give birth or to care for a baby. The Salvation Army and various religious communities opened hospitals where unmarried women could give birth and later homes where they could care for their baby in the initial weeks or arrange for an adoption.[19] Figures from the Salvation Army Hospital founded in 1890 showed about 20% of those who used the hospital were prostitutes, while the rest were women who 'got into trouble'.

The newly developed birth control movement of the early twentieth century repeatedly explained that birth control did not include abortion. Reagan draws on the correspondence sent to Mary Sanger's first birth control clinics in the USA in the 1920s to show that many women assumed it did include helping them facilitate an early abortion. 'The popular tradition of women did not make a distinction between contraception and abortion but saw them as part of the same project – a way to avoid unwanted childbearing.'[20] One argument for legitimizing contraception was that it could potentially end the need for abortions. Yet this needed to be put alongside the fear that it would promote extramarital sexual relationships. Birth control clinics argued that contraception was being offered to married couples as a way of maintaining smaller families. This would reduce abortions procured by women who already had children and did not feel they could cope with another one.

In Szreter's research, he identifies the Anglican clergy as a profession that appeared to successfully limit the size of their families, most probably through a limited form of abstinence.[21] Sexual continence could be seen as a Christian virtue, controlling sexual desire for the sake of the wife and the financial wellbeing of the family. As noted above, there was also a concern from those who, responding to the work of Thomas Malthus, feared an increasing population growth. This fear often linked to concerns about who was having the most children and whether contraception needed to be encouraged among those seen as the more indigent members of society. There were strong connections between those advocating for birth control and eugenic thinkers. Some of these concerns were taken up by certain Church of England bishops. A small number began to advocate for a change in the Anglican stance on the use of contraception. They suggested a pragmatic acceptance of contraception to help married couples plan their families responsibly; this could be viewed as a moral choice where abstinence was difficult to maintain. How these ideas changed the teaching of the Anglican Church can be seen by looking at resolutions from the Lambeth Conference. This conference brought together bishops from across the Anglican communion, including the USA, every ten years.

At the conference in 1908, it was affirmed that sex was given by God principally for procreation and so using contraception was morally wrong. At the delayed 1920 conference, Resolution 68 maintained the same view, stating:

> We utter an emphatic warning against the use of unnatural means for the avoidance of conception, together with the grave dangers – physical, moral and religious – thereby incurred, and against the evils with which the extension of such use threatens the race.[22]

The resolution mentioned that the primary purpose for which marriage exists is 'the continuation of the race through the gift and heritage of children', and opposed 'the teaching which, under the name of science and religion, encourages married people in the deliberate cultivation of sexual union as an end in itself'. However, in 1930, a resolution was passed that permitted the use of contraception if abstinence was not possible.

> Where there is clearly felt moral obligation to limit or avoid parenthood, the method must be decided on Christian principles. The primary and obvious method is complete abstinence from intercourse (as far as may be necessary) in a life of discipline and self-control lived in the power of the Holy Spirit. Nevertheless, in those cases where there is such a clearly felt moral obligation to limit or avoid parenthood, and where there is a morally sound reason for avoiding complete abstinence, the Conference agrees that other methods may be used, provided that this is done in the light of the same Christian principles. The Conference records its strong condemnation of the use of any methods of conception control from motives of selfishness, luxury, or mere convenience.[23]

The continuing promotion of abstinence linked to a spiritually disciplined life is held to be the better option, but now the couple can decide, on their Christian principles, that some form of contraception could be used to limit or avoid pregnancy. The Conference speaks positively of God's holy gift of sexual intercourse within marriage. In resolution 18, it states clearly that: 'Sexual intercourse between persons who are not legally married is a grievous sin. The use of contraception does not remove the sin.' It suggests that the sale or advertising of contraception should be severely restricted. It also makes it clear in resolution 16 that a cautious approval of contraception does not alter the view of abortion, recording the 'abhorrence of the sinful practice of abortion'.[24]

Other Protestant Churches followed the Anglican lead and a shift in a Christian attitude to contraception began.[25] The 1930s also saw a significant improvement in the production of condoms, as liquid latex made them cheaper and easier to use.[26] Managing family size through abstinence and through contraception was now seen as respectable. However, this was firmly resisted by the Roman Catholic Church. The Papal Encyclical *Casti Conubii* released later in 1930 reaffirmed a strongly Augustinian understanding of the procreative purpose of sex:

> Since, therefore, the conjugal act is destined primarily by nature for the begetting of children, those who in exercising it deliberately frustrate its natural power and purpose sin against nature and commit a deed that is shameful and intrinsically vicious.[27]

Use of contraception is described as 'an offense against the law of God and of nature, and those who indulge in such are branded with the guilt of a grave sin'.[28] There were dissenting voices within the Anglican and other Protestant Churches warning that giving even a tentative green light to contraception would increase sex outside of marriage, as it removed the fear of pregnancy. In this they were correct. The fear of pregnancy was a clear motivation for abstaining from premarital sexual intercourse, affecting both men and women. The man feared being forced to marry a girl he had got pregnant; the woman feared having a child outside of marriage.

## Legalizing abortion

While birth control in the form of contraception was being advocated and distanced from abortion, abortions continued to happen. The financial troubles of the 1930s played a part in decisions to terminate pregnancies, either to limit family size or to hold on to jobs for unmarried women. Finances would also play a part in access to safe abortion. Stephen Brookes states: 'there was a clear class divide between the availability of safe therapeutic abortion (curettage) and the more dangerous use of abortifacient pills, nonsurgical implements such as crochet hooks and knitting needles, and "folk" remedies such as slippery elm bark.'[29]

In 1936, the Abortion Law Reform Association was founded

in the UK, shaped by socialist feminism. It was principally motivated by the inequality that enabled those with money to access both contraception and safe abortion, while working-class women faced the risks of too many births or unsafe abortion, both of which could be fatal. 'During the 1930s, the unreliability of and inaccessibility of many forms of legal contraception left abortion as a weapon, albeit a dangerous one, against the threat of poverty.'[30] While infant mortality was falling, the rate of maternal death was stubbornly high. A UK Government inquiry into maternal mortality in 1937 noted that illegal abortions were a significant factor. This led to an inquiry into abortion, set up in 1937, reporting in 1939. It recognized that 'the law relating to abortion was freely disregarded among women of all types and classes', and that economic and financial reasons were the leading causes.[31] However, they did not recommend legalization of abortion as it would destroy the 'religious and ethical teaching and ... fundamental principles on which society is based'.[32] The opposition for legalizing abortion was based on fear of increased sexual promiscuity. It was sexual freedom, particularly on the part of women, that concerned the opponents, not language about protection of the unborn.

Brooke notes that the inquiry committee could not recognize the complexity of the evidence presented and opted for a simplistic understanding of abortion as a product of promiscuity or careerism. The Abortion Law Reform Association (ALRA) was set up by Stella Browne, Janet Chance and Alice Jenkins. Brooke maintains that the ALRA connected abortion to maternalism, to the ability of women to make good maternal decisions. Rather than seeing abortion as a threat to motherhood it was a way of family planning. They advocated for voluntary and responsible parenthood, equating abortion with other forms of birth control. Brooke quotes one of its members, Jane Chance:

> this Association deplores irresponsible behaviour with its consequences in shallow experience, illegitimacy and venereal disease, and it holds that one of the first ways of promoting

responsible sexual behaviour of fine and enduring quality is to make marriage more tolerable.[33]

Making marriage more tolerable meant reducing the concerns about multiple pregnancies with all of the financial and health implications. Brooke notes that, in England in the 1930s, 'the radicalism of abortion advocacy lay in the manner in which maternalism was invested with other meanings, such as citizenship, control, and autonomy'.[34] Reagan contrasts the US, where a feminist socialist challenge to abortion provision did not exist, and it would take the second wave of feminism to make abortion an issue. This would be more focused on women's autonomy and rights, and a concern that motherhood limited women. In the work of the ALRA, Brooke notes that the concept of maternalism was more expansive and less restrictive: women wanted to be mothers, but also wanted to be able to control how many children they had and when they had them; these were maternal decisions. It will be interesting to return to this idea of maternal decisions and abortion in Chapter 3.

The outbreak of World War Two meant that the question of legalizing abortion was on hold, and it would not be until the 1950s that the ALRA began seriously campaigning again. Between 1951 and 1966, three private members' bills (PMBs) were put forward in the UK to liberalize abortion laws, but all failed. Reports into maternal deaths in 1952 and 1966 showed that the leading cause of maternal death was now unsafe abortion. The introduction of antibiotics had reduced puerperal fever, which had been a major cause of maternal death. Finally, in 1967 a PMB introduced by the Liberal MP David Steel was passed, legalizing abortion under certain criteria if two doctors agreed. In 2001, King's College London organized a reunion of some of the key players involved in campaigning for the Act. Dr Paintin was one of the doctors; he recalls working in obstetrics and gynaecology in Bristol in the 1950s. Each day, Bristol General Hospital was admitting up to ten women with pain and bleeding in early pregnancy, who were having incomplete miscarriages mostly because of illegal abortions. He moved to work with Professor Dugald Baird in Aberdeen and found that he was regularly performing abortions as part of his NHS surgery. He simply scheduled two or three terminations at the end of each day's operating list for poor women who could not cope with another child. The Offences Against the Persons Act 1861 did not apply in Scotland and, although abortion was illegal, he was confident that he would not be prosecuted. His practice meant that in Aberdeen in areas of deprivation, families were smaller, children healthier and there was a reduction in maternal complications from multiple pregnancies.[35] Paintin says: 'By the time I left Aberdeen, I was convinced that a doctor could provide abortion ethically, and that safe abortion in an NHS hospital was preferable to clandestine abortion in the back streets.'[36] What was clear then, as now, is that abortion can be a safe procedure. The large number of complications and fatalities were from unsafe practices and infections from non-clinical settings.

From a religious perspective, the Anglican Church alongside other Churches continued to reflect on issues of sex, contraception and abortion. In 1958, the Lambeth Conference met again and reminded couples in resolution 113 that 'sexual love is not an end in itself nor a means to self-gratification, and that self-discipline and restraint are essential conditions of the freedom of marriage and family planning'.[37] Resolution 115 stated that:

> the responsibility for deciding upon the number and frequency of children has been laid by God upon the consciences of parents ... Such responsible parenthood, built on obedience to all the duties of marriage, requires a wise stewardship of the resources and abilities of the family as well as a thoughtful consideration of the varying population needs and problems of society and the claims of future generations.[38]

Samira Mehta maintains that this concept of responsibility was developed in mainline Protestant Churches into a form of Christian duty, especially in the 1960s with the development of the pill. 'Mainline Protestants came to frame birth control as the Christian obligation of responsible parenthood.' She states that married couples could:

> prayerfully make 'responsible' decisions about how many children to have based on societal concerns about the health of the planet, their ability to provide for those children without burdening society, and the number of children they had the emotional capacity to nurture.[39]

In 1965, the Church Assembly of the Church of England's Board of Social Responsibility published a report entitled *Abortion: an Ethical Discussion*. This report maintained that there might be circumstances in which abortion could be justified. They noted that the life and wellbeing of the mother was a key aspect of this justification, as was the wellbeing of her family. It was assumed in the report that a mixture of medics and social workers would need to assess each request. This was not a decision to be trusted to the woman herself. Gill notes that this document introduced a gradualist notion of the development of life in the womb, utilizing the language of potential person.

> It is possible to argue ... that between the moment of conception and the full maturity of the personality – whenever that may be assumed to have attained – there is a long period of development, and that the degree of protection which is this person's due develops *pari passu* with it.[40]

John Habgood, who later became Archbishop of York, had been key in developing this gradualist position. He stressed the importance of relationship to personhood, an idea that will be explored more fully in the next chapter. Reflecting on this, he wrote:

> The state at which an expectant mother begins to relate consciously to the foetus in her womb no doubt varies greatly with individuals, but the first consciously felt movements

have always been a significant landmark: this is why quickening was traditionally regarded as the point abortion was forbidden.[41]

Commenting on the ethical importance of this gradualist position, Robin Gill shows how it has been utilized in later discussions about IVF, embryo and stem-cell research. The fact that the established Church had given a cautious green light to legalized abortion was helpful in the progress of the 1967 Act.

In the reunion discussions remembering the passing of the 1967 Act, the politicians note the strong opposition from their Roman Catholic constituents. In their view, abortion was wrong and, despite the petitioning of many Roman Catholics, Vatican II did not change the position on contraception. Both contraception and abortion were seen to deliberately act against the procreative purpose of sex. The encyclical *Humanae Vitae* of 1968 picks up on the terminology of responsible parenting, which it affirms in principle. Yet is clear that this does not equate to using artificial means to prevent pregnancy.

> We are obliged once more to declare that the direct interruption of the generative process already begun and, above all, all direct abortion, even for therapeutic reasons, are to be absolutely excluded as lawful means of regulating the number of children. ... Similarly excluded is any action which either before, at the moment of, or after sexual intercourse, is specifically intended to prevent procreation – whether as an end or as a means.[42]

## Legal abortion

Making abortion legal in the UK, and free on the NHS, reduced maternal complications from poorly performed abortions and reduced maternal fatalities. Reflecting on the period after the passing of the Act, Dr Paintin notes that by 1972, emergency admissions for incomplete abortion/miscarriages had declined to about a third of 1962's admissions. By 1977, death resulting from an illegal abortion in England and Wales had ceased. 'Women were not terminating pregnancies they would have continued before the Act but were benefitting from safe legal abortions that otherwise they would have felt compelled to obtain illegally and with considerable danger to themselves.'[43] In New York State, USA, maternal mortality fell 45% the year after the state legalized abortion and septic abortion wards were closed.[44] In the last 30 years, 60 countries have liberalized abortion laws, but only Canada has fully decriminalized it. It is still a criminal offence in England and Wales to attempt to abort a pregnancy outside the limits of the Offences Against The Person Act 1861 and there have been concerns about an increase in investigations into some late miscarriages/stillbirths. Different reasons, and different gestational limits, apply where abortion is legal.

Access to legal abortion saves women's lives, and this is seen across the world today. A WHO report in 2022 gives a figure of 5–13% of maternal deaths as attributable to unsafe abortions. That rises steeply in poorer countries where abortion is illegal. Safe abortion in the first trimester has become increasingly managed by drugs. The development of misoprostol and mifepristone in the 1980s mean that an early miscarriage can be safely induced in the first trimester of pregnancy. Although in many countries they are meant to be taken in a clinic under medical supervision, there are no clear medical reasons for this. Increasingly, women are taking them at home and managing their own pregnancy ending. This has been increased by the experience of Covid-19 restrictions, where more women were sent medication to self-manage. Women's groups, such as *Women on the Web*, send the drugs into countries with abortion restrictions where women can self-administer and often provide emotional support from women, accompanying them through the subsequent pregnancy loss.

In some countries, there has been a backlash associating abortion with a challenge to the concept of the 'traditional family'. This mainly aligns with religious views from both

## HOW DO WE TALK ABOUT ABORTION?

Catholic and conservative evangelicals who express a concern for the rights of the unborn. Their anti-abortion stance has found allies in right-wing politicians concerned about immigration and fears of national population decline. Nicaragua, Poland, El Salvador and the USA have all moved to limit or ban abortion. Although abortion is legal in some countries, the cost is high, pricing out people from poorer backgrounds. The Reproductive Justice movement began in the USA to raise the concerns of African American women. The organization SisterSong defines reproductive justice 'as the human right to maintain personal bodily autonomy, have children, not have children, and parent the children we have in safe sustainable communities.'[45] While reproductive justice retains the language of rights in defending access to abortion, it sites this within an understanding of responsible maternity. Access to safe abortion needs to be set alongside access to contraception, good-quality sex education, adequate pre- and postnatal care, and financial support for those bringing up children. It also needs to address issues of domestic violence and safe homes.

The development of hormonal contraception has in many ways removed contraception from the act of sex. Whereas condoms are used during sex, the pill, intrauterine devices, hormonal patches and injections are all ways that women maintain a period of infertility, during which they might have sex. This places the responsibility for contraception firmly on women. They have to consider the risks of pregnancy while also considering any long-term medical risks of hormonal contraceptives. Delaying children until the circumstances are right is seen to be responsible family planning. So, a woman may use hormonal contraception to prevent pregnancy while she waits for the right partner or waits for her partner to commit to their future. She, or they, need enough resources to provide for the child, and this may also mean waiting for an appropriate point to take a career break. The costs of pregnancy and motherhood are taken seriously. Families are smaller, and the expectations of the demands of parenting are much higher. However, while waiting, they may not want to rule out any sexual relationships; the days of the majority of people considering sexual abstinence as a virtue have mainly gone. As noted in the last chapter, many mainline Churches have accepted that consensual sex in committed relationships before marriage is different from promiscuity and not to be condemned.

Marriage, like pregnancy, is often delayed until the finances are right and may come after the birth of children. Finances, careers and emotional resources will all impact on how many children make up a complete family. The birth rate is falling in the UK as in many developed countries, even countries with predominantly Roman Catholic populations. Contraception is used by many to space children and to limit the number. Vasectomies for men or tubal ligatures for women are a more permanent way of preventing conception, usually when a family is considered complete. Marital breakdown means that more men and women are single post-children and looking for relationships, whether casual or permanent. Navigating contraception post-children, and particularly during the perimenopause when periods become less regular, may be a necessary part of exploring new relationships. Statistics show a rise in abortions in the over-35s, which may indicate that contraception does not always work. Preventing pregnancy through contraception and, if that fails, abortion is likely to be the woman's responsibility. Although, it is interesting to see that an increase in vasectomies has followed the tightening of abortion laws in some parts of the US.[46]

In a previous article, I have characterized the mainline Church view on abortion, particularly the Church of England's statements, as 'You can if you must, but we would rather you didn't.' This position recognizes the need to ensure access to safe abortions although it hopes that these will be rare. It also recognizes that there may be circumstances where it would be unconscionable to expect a woman to continue a pregnancy. Yet, the assumption is that continuing a pregnancy should always be encouraged. This ties in with the language that abortion should be 'safe, legal and rare'. This impacts on how women may narrate the abortions that they do have. We note that women will often seek to explain that their abortion is exceptional, and from their perspective it may well appear that way. However, as will be discussed in the last chapter, women tend not to speak about their abortions for fear that others will not consider their reasons for making the choice sufficiently exceptional.

## How do we talk about abortion?

In talking about abortion, it is important to recognize that women have struggled with issues of infertility, pregnancy loss and unintended pregnancies throughout history. Having a child in the wrong circumstances has been burdensome and often radically altered a woman's life opportunities. Having too many children is physically stressful and can make it hard to care adequately for the children you have. Women have sought abortions in the hope of being able to mother well. This chapter has taken a brief look at the history of attitudes to contraception and abortion. Earlier understandings of biology and observations of spontaneous miscarriage in early pregnancy meant that the line between preventing a conception and ending an early pregnancy was less clearly drawn than in today's world. Irregular menstruation, uncertainty about the reasons for late or missed periods and the experience of miscarriage meant that the early stages of pregnancy were unpredictable. The notion that at this stage the foetus was unformed and theologically not yet ensouled made sense. At some point in the fourth or fifth month of pregnancy, the woman begins to feel her baby moving, known as 'quickening'. Ending a pregnancy before quickening, while never condoned, was considered less serious than aborting a child post-quickening. Like the use of contraception, it was seen as a violation of the purpose of sex, which was to procreate, rather than the taking of a life. High infant mortality and high maternal mortality meant that, for most married women, the concern was to have children that survived. Thus, contraception and abortion were associated with extramarital and thus unsanctioned sex, particularly prostitution.

The removal of quickening from the law concerning abortion in both the USA and UK was encouraged by doctors who did not trust women's observations of their pregnancies. The Offences Against the Person Act 1861 in England and Wales criminalized abortion at all stages of pregnancy, as did similar laws in the USA. Therapeutic abortion to save the life of a mother was within the law. Despite making early abortion criminal, women still sought ways to end unwanted pregnancies. As infant mortality began to fall significantly in the late nineteenth and early twentieth century, many of those seeking abortions were married mothers who wanted to limit the size of their family and to avoid another risky pregnancy and labour. Those with money and contacts could procure safe surgical procedures with no adverse consequences. Others resorted to various potions and poisons, physical interventions of their own or unsafe abortions provided by back-street abortionists. The consequences of these could be incomplete abortions, damage to the womb and other internal organs, and sepsis. These could prove fatal.

The birth control movement aimed to remove the stigma of contraception, which was associated with prostitution, and encourage married couples to use methods to limit their family size. They drew a firm line between contraception and abortion, which had to be constantly reiterated, as the popular understanding of early abortion was that it *was* a way of managing family size and preventing more risky pregnancies and childbirth. The Anglican Church's cautious endorsement of contraception as a part of responsible family planning was followed by other Protestant mainline Churches. As the 1958 Lambeth Conference stated it was for the couple to take responsibility for managing the size of their family. The Catholic Church maintained the link between sex and procreation, insisting that anything to deliberately prevent conception was contrary to God's will. By the mid-nineteenth century, any sense of delayed ensoulment had been rejected, with Pope Pius IX stating unequivocally that the soul enters the body at the moment of conception; thus, abortion at any point involves taking the life of an ensouled human.

The inequality of access to safe illegal abortions in the UK during the first half of the twentieth century and the high fatality rate from unsafe abortions motivated a challenge to the law. Feminist socialists argued that access to safe abortion was not contrary to promoting motherhood and family values, but would actually help women to make good responsible decisions about family size, affordability and welfare. Abortion should be part of responsible family planning, they argued, enabling women to make decisions about whether they could care for a new child at this time. The ALRA was joined by doctors and politicians who were horrified by the level of suffering and fatalities from unsafe abortions at a time when safe abortions could be easily provided. The Church of England again offered a cautious green light to legal abortion in exceptional circumstances. The 1967 Abortion Law allowed women access to free abortion if two doctors agreed that this was in the interest of their physical and mental health. The Church of England utilized a gradualist approach to the life in the womb in contrast to the Catholic position. However, they maintained the distinction between contraception, a responsible form of birth control, and abortion, an occasionally necessary procedure that was not part of family planning.

Modern forms of contraception and fertility treatment have added new complexities to the lines between prevention, abortion and early foetal life. Some forms of contraception act to prevent the implantation of a fertilized egg in the womb, while some hormonal contraceptives have this as a backup if the main aim of preventing ovulation has failed. The Catholic Church is clear that these are abortifacients and, if knowingly used, judges them as akin to procuring an abortion. The 'morning after pill', while not deliberately ending a known pregnancy, is aiming to prevent one that might happen. Most Protestant Churches do not take a view on this issue, and following the 'gradualist' view of life in the womb, they are supportive of IVF, even if embryos may be destroyed in the process. They are also supportive of stem-cell research. One of the concerns raised in the USA over strict anti-abortion legislation, which defines the embryo and foetus as a child from the moment of conception, is where this leaves fertility processes such as these.

Since the late twentieth century, contraception has become more effective and more available, but it is not without its problems. The human factor can impact how well contraception is used, and all forms of contraception have some failure rates. A 2021 Government survey showed that 50% of those accessing an abortion were using contraception.[47] In discussions around abortion, these facts need to be recognized. Drawing tight lines between contraception as a responsible act and abortion as irresponsible is not helpful. Today, abortion is mainly used to end a pregnancy in its early months by inducing a miscarriage. This happens before the baby's movements are felt and before others can see the pregnancy. These early months of pregnancy are when most miscarriages happen.

The next chapter will look at early pregnancy abortions ending unintended pregnancies alongside the experience of spontaneous pregnancy loss. Reclaiming the language of responsible parenting can provide a more constructive way of talking about abortion than discussions of rights. This is then not about a woman asserting her rights over the rights of an unborn baby; it is about considering whether she can accept the responsibility for bringing a child into the circumstances she lives in, given that she would be the mother of the child and society would hold her responsible for its wellbeing.

## Notes

1 Michael Kandiah and Gillian Staerck, eds, 2002, *The Abortion Act 1967*, London: Institute of Contemporary British History, p. 39.

2 Leslie J. Reagan, 1997, *When Abortion Was a Crime: Women, Medicine, and Law in the United States, 1867–1973*, Berkeley: University of California Press, pp. 140–1.

3 'Reproductive Justice', https://www.sistersong.net/reproductive-justice, accessed 01.05.2025.

4 Helen King, 1998, *Hippocrates' Woman: Reading the Female Body in Ancient Greece*, London: Routledge, p. 134.

5 Islamic scholars still follow a theory of delayed ensoulment, which allows early terminations to be less problematic. Jewish theologians have traditionally read this passage to show that the developing life in the womb is not yet a person; instead, human life begins at birth when the child breathes their first breath.

6 John M. Riddle, 1998, *Eve's Herbs: A History of Contraception and Abortion in the West*, Cambridge, MA: Harvard University Press.

7 King, *Hippocrates' Woman*, pp. 145–6.

8 King, *Hippocrates' Woman*, p. 139.

9 King, *Hippocrates' Woman*, p. 142.

10 Katharine Park, 2018, 'Managing Childbirth and Fertility in Medieval Europe', in Nick Hopwood, Rebecca Fleming and Lauren Kassell, eds, *Reproduction: Antiquity to the Present Day*, Cambridge: Cambridge University Press, p. 163.

11 Park, 'Managing Childbirth', p. 165.

12 Park, 'Managing Childbirth', pp. 163–6.

13 https://www.shbb.org/, accessed 01.05.2025.

14 Reagan, *When Abortion Was a Crime*, p. 8.

15 Reagan, *When Abortion Was a Crime*, p. 13.

16 Reagan, *When Abortion Was a Crime*, p. 54.

17 Simon Szreter, 1996, *Fertility, Class and Gender in Britain, 1860–1940*, Cambridge Studies in Population, Economy, and Society in Past Time 27, Cambridge/New York: Cambridge University Press.

18 Szreter, *Fertility, Class and Gender*, p. 396.

19 Pat Thane, 2012, *Sinners? Scroungers? Saints? Unmarried Motherhood in Twentieth-Century England*, Oxford: Oxford University Press, p. 26.

20 Reagan, *When Abortion Was a Crime*, p. 41.

21 Szreter, *Fertility, Class and Gender*, p. 410.

22 'Lambeth Conference', 1920, https://www.anglicancommunion.org/resources/document-library.aspx?author=Lambeth+Conference&year=1920, accessed 01.05.2025.

23 'Lambeth Conference', 1930, https://www.anglicancommunion.org/resources/document-library.aspx?author=Lambeth+Conference&year=1930, accessed 01.05.2025.

24 'Lambeth Conference', 1930.

25 Samira Mehta, 2018, 'Family Planning Is a Christian Duty: Religion, Population Control, and the Pill in the 1960s', in Gillian Frank, Bethany Moreton and Heather R. White (eds), *Devotions and Desires: Histories of Sexuality and Religion in the Twentieth-Century United States*, p. 152.

26 Szreter, *Fertility, Class and Gender*, p. 435.

27 Pope Pius XI, 1930, *Casti Connubii: On Christian Marriage*, Vatican Press, para. 54, https://www.vatican.va/content/pius-xi/en/encyclicals/documents/hf_p-xi_enc_19301231_casti-connubii.html, accessed 01.05.2025.

28  Pope Pius XI, *Casti Connubii*, para. 56.

29  Stephen Brooke, 2001, '"A New World for Women"? Abortion Law Reform in Britain during the 1930s', *The American Historical Review* 106(2) (April), p. 441, https://doi.org/10.2307/2651613, accessed 01.05.2025.

30  Brooke, '"A New World for Women"?', p. 441.

31  Quoted in Brooke, '"A New World for Women"?', p. 457.

32  Brooke, '"A New World for Women"?', p. 457.

33  Brooke, '"A New World for Women"?', p. 448.

34  Brooke, '"A New World for Women"?', p. 443.

35  Jonathan Brown, 2022, 'Decriminalising Abortion: Challenges for Scotland', https://www.strath.ac.uk/humanities/lawschool/blog/decriminalisingabortionchallengesforscotland, accessed 01.05.2025.

36  Kandiah and Staerck, *The Abortion Act 1967*, p. 43.

37  Lambeth Conference Resolutions Archive, 1958, Resolution 113, https://www.anglicancommunion.org/media/127740/1958.pdf, accessed 01.05.2025

38  Lambeth Conference Resolutions Archive, 1958, Resolution 115

39  Mehta, 'Family Planning', p. 153.

40  Church of England, Church of England Information Office, and Church of England Central Board of Finance, 1965, *Abortion: An Ethical Discussion*, [London]: Published for The Church Assembly Board for Social Responsibility by the Church Information Office, p. 29.

41  Quoted in Robin Gill, 2021, 'Church of England (Anglican) Perspectives on Abortion', in Alireza Bagheri, ed., *Abortion: Global Positions and Practices, Religious and Legal Perspectives*, Cham: Springer International Publishing, pp. 63–72.

42  Pope Paul VI, 1968, *Humanae Vitae: On the Regulation of Human Births*, Vatican Press, https://www.papalencyclicals.net/paul06/p6humana.htm, accessed 01.05.2025.

43  Kandiah and Staerck, *The Abortion Act 1967*, p. 46.

44  Reagan, *When Abortion Was a Crime*, p. 246.

45  'Reproductive Justice', https://www.sistersong.net/reproductive-justice, accessed 01.05.2025.

46  Tara Haelle, 2024, 'More Men Are Getting Vasectomies', *Scientific American*, https://www.scientificamerican.com/article/more-men-are-getting-vasectomies-since-roe-was-overturned/, accessed 01.05.2025.

47  UK Department of Health and Social Care, 2025, 'Women's Reproductive Health Survey 2021 National Pilot: Contraception and Abortion Results', https://www.gov.uk/government/publications/womens-reproductive-health-survey-2021-national-pilot-contraception-and-abortion-results/a048d786-8ea4-4a10-808b-8b0311f2f1d2, accessed 01.05.2025.

# 3

# Unintended Pregnancy and Early Abortion

When my son was about eight years old, he overheard a conversation I was having about a friend trying to make a decision about an unintended pregnancy. This individual thought she had completed her family, and there were complex financial and familial concerns about adding another child at this time. She had conceived accidentally. How, my son asked me, did she not know she was having sex? I had to explain that sex isn't just about making a baby. The sex was intended, but the pregnancy was not. Abortions happen in many circumstances for just this reason. Sexual relations happen within and outside committed relationships. We know that women engage in sex joyfully, willingly, thoughtfully and carelessly. It is also important to remember, as mentioned previously, that a woman does not need to be aroused for a man to have penetrative vaginal sex with her and for that sex to result in pregnancy. This means that women also have sex through manipulation, coercion and force. Questions of consent in terms of sex are, quite rightly, a matter of serious concern and debate. The consequence for a woman who unintentionally becomes pregnant is far more complex than for the man who impregnated her. This is an issue about women's bodies and women's lives.

If a woman who finds herself pregnant is morally obliged to continue the pregnancy and birth a child, then it has been assumed that the consent to sex was also a provisional consent to pregnancy. Restricting sexual relations to situations where the possibility of pregnancy is accepted has been a central feature of Christian moral teaching, connecting consent to sex to consent to pregnancy for a woman. The fear of an unintended conception and the life-changing consequences of bearing a child in inauspicious circumstances has been a means of controlling women's sexual behaviour, particularly before reliable contraception. It also affected male behaviour; an unintended pregnancy might mean a requirement to marry. While the Church has always taught that children are a gift from God, the attitude to children born outside of conventional relationships has not been welcoming. Social and religious stigma caused judgement to be passed on such women and children. Men's sexual misdemeanours do not carry the same consequences and have been viewed as less serious. Social and religious stigmatizing of unintended pregnancies does not always consider whether the sex was manipulated, coerced or forced. Through their own choices, and through the behaviour of others, both in and outside committed relationships, women become pregnant when they did not intend to have a child. They are faced with the knowledge that they have conceived, and the beginning of a new life is gestating within their womb.

A stance against abortion assumes that a woman should live with the consequences of her behaviour. Under this view, to have sex is to be open to the possibility of conceiving a child. As noted in the previous chapter, Roman Catholic teaching continues to connect sex and procreation. Each sexual encounter should hold together an act of love with the possibility of procreation. This means that Roman Catholicism prohibits the use of contraception as well as abortion, as both stop procreation. Less emphasis is placed on the problem of sex without love. The majority of mainline Churches recognize that sex is valuable in a relationship even when procreation is not intended. The last chapter showed the change in attitude to contraception. This also changed the attitude to having children, becoming one where responsible parenting means family planning. The changes in sexual behaviour in the latter part of the twentieth century have continued to prioritize sex for pleasure, though it is not always clear that the pleasure is mutual.

## HOW DO WE TALK ABOUT ABORTION?

The use of contraception within committed and casual relationships has reduced the number of unintended pregnancies and enabled many couples to control the size of their family. It has altered sexual behaviour; however, use of contraception is not 100% reliable and those using it do not always understand its limitations. Unintended pregnancies can happen due to contraceptive failures. There can also be problems in accessing contraception, and medical or cultural reasons why it is not always used. Hormonal contraceptive pills or devices can have difficult side effects for the women taking them. Chaotic lives, bouts of illness and simple forgetfulness play a part in unreliable contraceptive use. Some men dislike using condoms and make it hard for women to insist on their use. The promotion of contraception as a sensible way of planning pregnancy needs to acknowledge the possibility of failure. Ann Furedi challenges the narrative of good responsible contraception and bad immoral abortion. 'Despite doctors' best intentions, contraception has never replaced abortion. It may *lessen* the need for abortions and thus reduce the abortion rate. But the inconvenient truth remains: contraception sometimes fails and people sometimes fail to use it.'[1]

In the UK, the statistics for England and Wales show that the trend for abortions in the under 18s has been going down over the last 10 years, as have teenage pregnancy rates. Scotland has seen a small rise in this age group, but these are still a small proportion of the overall figures. There is a steady increase in abortions for those over 35 years, although these too represent a small proportion. The rate is highest for those in their early twenties. In England and Wales, 18% of people having an abortion stated that they were married; 51% gave their status as single with a partner. In 2022, those living in the most deprived areas of England were almost twice as likely to have an abortion than those living in the least deprived areas.[2] The figures for Scotland are similar.[3] As noted above, most abortions are carried out in the first trimester of pregnancy and most are terminating an unintended pregnancy.

## Pregnancy is costly

When a woman discovers that she is unintentionally pregnant, she needs to make a decision. She looks at her circumstances and considers what a full-term pregnancy and future child will require of her. Catriona McKenzie maintains this decision-making involves three stages of moral responsibility. First, there is 'causal responsibility' for the foetus held by the woman and the man whose combined egg and sperm have created it. They have started a developing life that, if not terminated, will become a new human being genetically related to each of them. This is not insignificant, binding them, at some level, to the life of a child if it is born. For the woman, the knowledge that she is pregnant leads to the second responsibility: to 'make a decision'. She may involve the father in this decision, or not, depending on their relationship. The primary decision responsibility must be the woman's because it is in her body that this life will develop. Her decision will be based not simply on the responsibility to the foetus but taking in the wider moral responsibilities she has.[4] If the decision is made to continue the pregnancy, then she has accepted 'parental responsibility', which is McKenzie's third stage. This responsibility will grow and deepen as the pregnancy continues. She has accepted this parental responsibility even if she is planning to have the baby adopted.

In talking about abortion, there needs to be an understanding of the costliness of pregnancy to a woman. A full-term pregnancy lasts for about 40 weeks and places physical, emotional, social and financial strains on her. For some women it can be fatal. Maternal death is still a reality, even in medically advanced countries, and there are concerning factors around race and poverty that increase the risks. During pregnancy, there are health risks ranging from dental and joint problems to diabetes and raised blood pressure. Extreme nausea can last for the first months or considerably longer. For many women, pregnancy and childbirth will have minor or more serious long-term health consequences beyond the pregnancy. Multiple pregnancies can increase the risks of complications and the long-term impact on a woman's body. In most societies, pregnancy significantly affects women's earning power and career prospects. The visibility of pregnancy in its latter stages makes it public, impacting on a woman's place in her community.

If a woman intends to be pregnant, then she accepts the costs involved in bringing this new life into the world. Without her bodily generosity, a baby cannot be born. She is not an incubator: her body doesn't simply hold the embryo/foetus; it actively sustains, nurtures and affects the development of this life. She is a co-creator. Her health, her emotional state, her diet, all play a part in the development. Medical science is continually learning more about the interaction between the mother and foetus during pregnancy. At no point can a woman share the burden of gestating this new life. She cannot take a break, hand over this pregnancy to someone who wants it, or stop it at the point someone declares the foetus to be viable. Too often discussions of abortion speak about the developing life as if it were separate from the woman. There is no living foetus that is not entirely dependent on the sustaining nurturing body of a woman. No child can be born that has not been gestated by a woman.

The decision to give her body to the making of a new person is consequential, life-changing. This new person will be her child. Tina Beattie writes: 'In a sense, pregnancy involves a double birth; the birth of a mother and the birth of a child.'[5] Reflecting on this momentous reality, some women feel that for many reasons they cannot make that commitment. If a woman decides that she does not feel able to give herself to the making of a child and being its mother, then having a safe legal abortion allows her, as Kamitsuka puts it, to 'end her mothering obligations early'. Ann Cahill describes the woman's first knowledge of the pregnancy as a call. 'The pregnant subject cannot escape or pre-empt the call of the other; nevertheless, she is able to respond to the call in a variety of ways.'[6] Beattie also uses the idea of a call and draws on the biblical imagery of the Annunciation. Mary's encounter with the angel

Gabriel records her assent to bearing this holy child. Her 'yes' is important, confirming her agency. She is not forced, and she could have said 'no'. Helen Oppenheimer urges caution because Mary's 'yes' has been held up as a model of obedience. 'If she refuses, Christians may think that she has refused an annunciation, that she has declined to say, "Be it unto me according to thy will": but her acceptance could hardly be praised unless her refusal were a possibility.'[7] Amy Peeler concurs:

> Gabriel's words include no alternative, no punishment or threat if she does not embrace this word. Without such a statement, if she rejects, she would miss out on the blessing of mothering the Messiah, but there is no threat of repercussion if she choose not to accept.[8]

Stressing a woman's agency in responding to the call to continue a pregnancy takes seriously the task facing her: to participate bodily in the making of a new human being and becoming its mother. But it is also important to consider who is calling. Is it God who ordains each conception? Where God is understood as the one who opens and shuts the womb, is each conception deliberately God given? Mary's assent came before she conceived. Her 'no', had she given it, would not have involved the ending of something that had already begun and for many that is the problem with abortion.

The philosopher Soran Reader maintains that, even when writing in support of abortion, it must be understood as a killing.[9] This is strong language that feels uncomfortable. Yet, I recognize her reasoning. It needs to be recognized that there is a developing life that will need to be deliberately ended if the pregnancy is terminated. This is not simply a bunch of cells to be removed, but a living embryo or foetus that could become a human baby. To acknowledge this is not to equate life at any stage automatically with personhood. The debates around the morality of abortion tend to focus on the status of this life and whether there is a moral duty to preserve it, even if the woman did not intend the pregnancy. There is a presumption that what is begun should continue because being born is a good thing, and what God intended. Yet, the woman has to decide whether it is good, not just for her but for the child she would be bringing into the world. Does what has been started have to be continued despite the circumstances? She may conclude that this is not the time or situation in which to gestate, birth and rear a child. While abstract discussions of the status of the gestating life have their place, for pregnant women the issue is always concrete: it is *this* beginning, *this* life. In the first trimester, this nascent life is not known, only known *about*, through bodily changes and medical confirmation.

Many conceptions are lost spontaneously. Talking about elective abortion in early pregnancy needs to be within the context of women's experience of pregnancy loss. Philosophy and theology written from the experience of miscarriage is helpful in doing this. The frequency of pregnancy loss challenges the presumption that it is God who ordains each conception. Human fertility appears to be fickler and more random than is often portrayed.

## Early pregnancy endings

The first trimester of pregnancy can be an unstable period. Spontaneous endings, miscarriages, happen at this stage for reasons that are still not fully understood. The journey of the fertilized egg into the womb is not guaranteed, and we do not know how many fail to implant and are expelled from the body within menstrual blood. When might a late period be an early loss of something conceived? We do know that one in five known pregnancies will end in a loss. In *The Dark Womb*, Karen O'Donnell reflects theologically on the experience of miscarriage and the challenge to traditional understandings of God's providence.

> There is something particularly problematic about believing that God has a divine plan for your life ... and thus that

God gives the gift of life to the baby you are carrying, even in those early days of pregnancy, if that pregnancy was only ever going to result in miscarriage. ... What kind of Divine Providence do we see at work in that experience?[10]

She goes on to say: 'Conception, pregnancy and birth are biological processes, not divine ones. ... God does not cause a person to become pregnant.' Not every conception becomes a born child, and for those who wanted the pregnancy, the sense of loss can be profound. Early pregnancy loss happens at a stage when the signs of pregnancy are not visible to those beyond the woman and her intimate partner. Many women, myself included, are encouraged to keep their pregnancy private until past 12 weeks because of the precarity of the pregnancy in those early months.

It is during this precarious time that most abortions are carried out. Medication can induce pregnancy loss akin to a spontaneous miscarriage. Two medications are taken, one to end the foetal life and the second to encourage the body to expel the pregnancy. This method of abortion is routinely carried out up to the tenth week of pregnancy. It is medically safe and, as with a spontaneous loss, has no impact on future pregnancies. It is usually possible for the woman to decide where to be when the pregnancy is lost and how to dispose of what is expelled from her body. Surgical intervention can also safely end a pregnancy. 'With modern medical knowledge, instruments and medication, it is neither difficult nor dangerous to end a pregnancy.'[11] At this early stage too, the pregnancy can be kept private.

Tina Beattie argues that the first weeks of pregnancy can be considered as a period of grace. She suggests that a woman may conceive biologically before she consciously accepts the pregnancy and, in that gap, she should be allowed to terminate a pregnancy she cannot embrace.[12] The idea of a grace period reflects this liminal time in early pregnancy, and it offers a very helpful understanding of the need for a woman to commit to the pregnancy. In the embodied experience of pregnancy, this is a strange time when you know you are pregnant, either from test results or from reading the subtle bodily changes, yet you do not yet have a sense of this life that is beginning and others cannot see that you are pregnant. For Beattie, this also reflects a gradualist view of the developing life. She notes that the foetus is at an early stage of development, and this is for her a factor in the permissibility of early abortion; she opposes abortion after 12 weeks' gestation. Pastorally, this period of grace is helpful in thinking about early abortion. It means that most early terminations could be considered to fall in this grace period. Yet, this gradualist position becomes more problematic when considering spontaneous pregnancy loss. Does it mean that the value of the foetus can be understood in terms of its developmental state and does this question the depth of grief for those who experience pregnancy loss in the early weeks?

As noted in the last chapter, there is a long tradition of differentiating between ending a pregnancy of what was termed an unformed or formed foetus, though much of this derives from faulty historic biology. Kamitsuka's overview of historic Christian thinking, referred to in the introduction, shows how questions of formation, ensoulment and the significance afforded to quickening, have been understood in the theological tradition.[13] It was also noted in the last chapter that this gradualist approach was used in Church of England support for legalizing abortion. It is an important aspect of pregnancy that the foetus develops. What begins as a cluster of cells develops into an embryo, a foetus and eventually a baby. Most countries hold different views about the status of these three stages. This is factored into legislation around abortion, fertility treatment, medical research and pregnancy loss.

Modern debates draw on modern understanding of biology, and medical observation, to consider the developmental stage of the foetus. Different milestones are given significance – a heartbeat, the development of the spinal cord, limbs, etc. – and we see this information used in legal restrictions on abortion. While the developmental stages can be observed, the significance for the personhood, capacity to feel or otherwise of the foetus is subjective. The stage of the foetal development does impact on the process of termination and what matter is passed. It also, as noted above, affects how the woman can limit the impact on her wider relationships by keeping the pregnancy private. However, developing a justification for termination by arguing that the early-stage foetus is disposable because it is so underdeveloped fails to take account of how women relate to a pregnancy loss. Women's understanding of the life in their womb is complex. Some will speak of an early loss as the loss of a baby; some will not. This is true for spontaneous and induced pregnancy loss. In talking about abortion, particularly from a pastoral perspective, the experience of those who have suffered miscarriage needs to be considered.

In 1995, I was delighted to be pregnant with what I assumed would be my second child. I had nausea but not as bad as the first time. I had positive pregnancy tests and recognizable bodily changes to tell me I was pregnant. At ten weeks I began to bleed. After a few days of steady but relatively light bleeding, I had an ultrasound scan. On the screen a tiny blob was found to have no heartbeat and had clearly stopped developing a few weeks before. This was technically called a missed miscarriage and I was taken in for surgery to remove the pregnancy. I was deeply upset; I wanted a second child. I was reassured that this was a common occurrence and encouraged to try again. Within three months, I was pregnant and subsequently my second child was born. What had I lost? I did not talk of the loss of a baby but of a potential baby. I did not feel I had developed a relationship. I had been waiting for the subtle movement from within, quickening that would begin to offer me a sense of the baby as a separate being. I still think of this as a lost pregnancy rather than a lost baby. I know that this is shaped by the birth of my second child. Had the first pregnancy gone to term, I would have had a different second child, not the one I know and love. Yet, I know that others have different ways of narrating a similar experience. For them, it is helpful to speak of a lost baby and even to name that baby.

There has been a growing awareness that the pastoral

response to pregnancy loss, especially in the early stages, has failed to recognize the depth of grief. The planned nature of many pregnancies, the fertility help that some women have and the increasing ability to peer into the womb through scans, all add to the lived experience of miscarriage as the loss of a baby. Many people find a mismatch between their sense of loss and the way it is understood, in practice, as a natural occurrence. My loss was recorded as a spontaneous abortion. This would not be the case for someone today. It became clear that seeing the word abortion in their notes, even modified by 'spontaneous' caused serious distress. Women associated it with a deliberate termination. Practice has been changed and the terminology is now to note a miscarriage. An early miscarriage is not registered as a death. A stillbirth is only recognized as such after 24 weeks of pregnancy in the UK (20 in the USA). It is only in recent times that what is lost can be disposed of reverently in some kind of funeral rather than as clinical waste. In 2024, the UK Government introduced a scheme that provides a 'baby loss certificate' on request to mark a pregnancy loss before 24 weeks. This can show the names of parents, the sex of the baby if known, a given name and the date of loss.[14] The demand for these certificates, which can record a historic pregnancy loss, has been high. The main charities that support women and their partners in such a loss use the language of baby loss; there is encouragement to name the baby and engage in personal grieving rituals. Churches have been slower to catch up with this change in practice, but annual baby loss services have become more frequent, including for those who have miscarried. O'Donnell's book *The Dark Womb* offers resources for prayers and rituals for those who have experienced miscarriage, and these have been welcomed and used by many.

If a miscarriage at under ten weeks of pregnancy is discussed as the loss of a baby, how does that impact on deliberate pregnancy endings at the same stage? At the outset, it is important to acknowledge the unfairness of the fertility lottery. Some women who really want to have children can't get pregnant. Some who get pregnant miscarry for reasons that are not understood. Some women get pregnant when they did not intend to, do not want to be and feel unable to commit to having a child. This means that a woman can lose her much-hoped-for baby at the same stage that another woman deliberately ends her pregnancy. What we must remember is that these are not interchangeable babies. The women facing pregnancy loss, spontaneous or deliberate, are unique, facing a particular set of circumstances, gestating a life begun in a particular sexual encounter. They will differ in how they think and talk about what is lost and how they narrate the loss for themselves and those they share the information with.

The philosopher Kate Parsons, as an advocate of women's right to terminate a pregnancy, had always used medical terms (embryo, foetus), but these did not seem appropriate for her own pregnancy loss. The literature that took her grief seriously encouraged her to speak of her baby. She writes: 'Did my conflicted feelings signal an inconsistency in, or at least a challenge for, pro-choice feminists?'[15] Her dilemma is summed up by another philosopher, K. Lindsay Chambers, in a paper titled 'It's Complicated'.[16] She maintains we need 'an account of foetal moral status that can explain why it is appropriate to love some foetuses but not others'. The dichotomy that Parsons and Chambers outline deals with concrete experience and pastoral realities. 'The important task, it seems, is not to determine whether the embryo/foetus is "real" and a "person" but to listen to why a woman might feel the need to insist on categorizing it as such in the first place.'[17]

Parsons calls for an understanding of personhood that acknowledges the different ways that women relate to their pregnancy:

> A relational model that recognizes the uniqueness of each woman's feelings and circumstances is important not just for the melding of pro-choice feminism with the diverse experiences of miscarriage, but also for the melding of pro-choice feminism with the experience of pregnancy and elective abortion.[18]

Women who experience early pregnancy loss differ in how they want to talk about what is lost. The fact that some find that grieving a 'baby' matches their sense of loss does not make this prescriptive. Women who terminate a pregnancy may also speak about their 'baby'.[19] Pastoral sensitivity is needed in listening to the experience of the woman. The stage of development does not predict the way the woman experiences her loss and how she narrates what has been lost. As Parsons argues, we need to note how the woman relates to the developing life within.

## Calling into personhood

The relationship between a woman and the life she is gestating is a moral category unlike any other. The developing life is entirely contingent on the woman. To explore the relational nature of pregnancy further, I draw on the work of Hilda Lindemann. She reminds us that:

> fetuses don't just grow into persons by themselves. They are the kind of things whose value resides in their ability to *become* persons, but it takes a woman to *get* them there. Pregnancy, then, isn't merely something that happens to a woman – it is something she does. It is misleading to think of pregnant women's bodies as flowerpots, ovens, incubators because when we do that, we lose sight of how pregnancy requires the exercise of a woman's moral agency.[20]

Lindemann proposes a social understanding of personhood. Through a process of recognition and response, we confer personhood on each other and hold it for each other. This recognition, and response, is embodied. This impacts on her understanding of the life in the womb.

Such a life is hidden, so the process of recognition and response cannot happen until the woman chooses to begin a relationship and 'call her fetus into personhood'. Lindemann writes:

what begins as a purely biological relationship is transformed into a recognizable human one because, by what the woman does in word, deed, and imagination, she calls her fetus into personhood. It's not until after she starts doing this that the fetus becomes the sort of entity with whom personal relations are even possible.'[21]

This is a proleptic relationship, for even the woman cannot see the baby or do more than surmise its life. She only has foetal movements from about 14 or 15 weeks onwards to use in beginning to assign some character. In my first pregnancy, I began to refer to the gestating life as 'Fidget' because I experienced a lot of foetal movement. This naming is an aspect of calling into personhood. The increased use of scans with accompanying pictures offers information to feed the proleptic relationship. This may reveal the sex of the baby, something of its size and shape. It is more common these days for people to tell you the given name of a baby before it has been born and to share the scan photos. Lindemann notes that this is 'a purely one-sided activity – the fetus hasn't yet developed the personality to which it will give bodily expression when born'.[22] The mother-to-be makes physical arrangements, creates social connections and thinks about it as if it were already the born child it will be. Once born, it is possible to begin an intersubjective relationship with a baby. All of the senses can now be drawn on to know this unique individual. Others join the mother in picking out family resemblances, in delighting in the smell and feel of this tiny infant. The baby now must make its needs known to those who care, no longer being able to rely on the constant sustenance given in the womb.

For feminist writers, the relational understanding of personhood that Lindemann presents provides a better expression of the unique experience of pregnancy than discussing foetal development, as if the life in the womb is experienced as it will be once born. Lindemann writes from a secular position, and theologians might respond that, because God sees and recognizes the developing life, God confers personhood. While

I acknowledge that God has a care and concern for all aspects of creation, I am still persuaded by the social nature of personhood that Lindemann outlines. Grounding the sense of personhood in this recognition and response is an important reminder of the inherent social nature of being human. As Elisabeth Moltmann-Wendal writes, 'we do not begin as monads but as beings in relationship, who are concerned ... to attain recognition and selfhood with one another and through one another'.[23] While the developing life of the early foetus can be acknowledged, the sense of personhood needs the recognition of another person in relationship. It is for the mother to begin to recognize the otherness developing within and contingent on her. It is understandable that in a planned pregnancy, a wanted pregnancy, this calling into personhood may begin very early as the woman anticipates the baby she longs for. Thus, her sense of loss will be shaped by this emotional investment. Yet, it also needs to be acknowledged that some women do not find this proleptic relationship easy and only really begin the relationship when the child is born.

When the pregnancy is unintended, the woman has to ask herself if she can invest in this relationship and call this person into being. I follow Reader and Kamitsuka in maintaining that women use maternal thinking to make their decision. They utilize their imagination to think what it would be like to be the mother of the child that would be born if this pregnancy continues. For some, this may lead them quickly to a decision to end the pregnancy. The idea of being the mother of a child with that father, a man who raped or abused, coerced or lied to her, is abhorrent. The child would be related to him; he might choose to claim some kind of parental rights. Would the child always remind her of the circumstances of the conception? How would this pregnancy be narrated to others? Would she have to expose herself and deeply traumatic events to public scrutiny? Reader writes:

> Where procreation is willed this contributes to the moral value of the foetus and makes the moral loss of the foetal

life greater. Where procreation is unwilled, in rape, for example, it is commonly agreed that pressure to continue with the pregnancy is more unjust. What is less commonly noticed is that the moral status of the foetus may be altered by the absence of consent to procreation.[24]

This is an important point. Laws around abortion consider gestational development and viability of the foetus in general terms. An exceptionalist position holds that the context of the pregnancy should also be considered: not 'Is this pregnancy viable?', but 'Is it right that this woman should be made to carry this child?' Reader concludes that the absence of consent not only absolves the mother of an obligation to continue the pregnancy, 'but that the absence of consent bestows a negative moral status on the foetus'. In such a case, it is understandable that a decision may be reached that says the foetus should not exist. This is not because a foetus is of no importance at this stage, but because *this* foetus should not have come into being. The issue is whether a woman should be obliged to continue a pregnancy in such circumstances because a conception has occurred. Churches that hold an exceptionalist rather than an absolute opposition to abortion tend to consider rape as grounds for an abortion. In accepting this contextual concern, there is a recognition that not all conceptions must be gestated to birth.

The circumstances of the conception may not be so traumatic. It may be the result of careless sex, failed contraception, or some other reason why the pregnancy was unintended. In such a case, the woman will still need to use her imagination to think about this potential child. What does a child require and can she provide it? These are emotional, financial, social and practical questions. Studies show that financial concerns figure in many decisions to terminate a pregnancy. Opposition to abortion is narrated as concern for the unborn child, yet we live in societies where many children are born into poverty and neglect. Rebecca Todd Peters comments on this:

> If we are truly concerned about the health and wellbeing of pregnant women and their children, then we ought to be addressing through our public policy the social problems that women cite as contributing to their decisions to terminate a pregnancy. ... we need to tackle the social problems themselves rather than punishing women for the responsible decisions they make within their social world.[25]

Choosing not to bring a child to birth into situations of violence, poverty or social exclusion is a reasonable decision and shows concern for the wellbeing of the potential child.

This raises again issues about seeing each conception as God's provision. If an unplanned pregnancy is narrated as God's gift, what is it saying about God's concern for the pregnant woman? For someone who is pregnant because of forced, coercive or manipulative sex, or even just because the condom split, the conception may be experienced as a punishment or a cruel joke rather than a gift. If this is God's doing, then why is God 'punishing' the woman for behaviour that she may not have had much agency in? Why, they may ask, does God think it good for a child to be born into a difficult, dangerous or damaging situation? This is not to suggest that a child born under such circumstances cannot be a blessing; there are women who have found a blessing in an unintended pregnancy even from the most difficult circumstances, and children born from difficult beginnings can flourish. Yet, we must also acknowledge that an unintended pregnancy can have a devastating impact on a woman's life and can have complex issues for the wellbeing of a born child. The general capacity of God's providence in our lives needs to be separated from the belief that God is controlling every aspect of our lives. For God to oversee and ordain each conception raises difficult issues about human agency, pregnancy loss and the deeply gendered cost of pregnancy. David Fergusson, writing on the providence of God, says: 'We may want to see every occasion as situated within the scope of God's care, but this is a different thought from the one that sees every event as sent by God.'[26]

In imagining the possibility of this pregnancy leading to the birth of a child, a woman will also need to factor in her current caring responsibilities particularly for other children. UK statistics show that over half of women accessing an abortion had previously had a child.[27] There is no information about how many of those children are being cared for by their birth mothers, but concern for other children was cited by over a quarter of those surveyed in the USA.[28] It may be that the woman currently has no children and has not envisioned having a child at this point in her life. Imagining how a pregnancy and subsequent child will impact on her education, career and long-term relationships should not be characterized as selfish. A child will alter her future choices and the role she plays in society. This task of imagining the child-that-might-be is a necessary aspect of the decision-making and reflects her agency and moral capacity. Some women may make decisions for reasons that others find unconvincing but that is true in many areas of life. Here the decision is whether she can imagine herself as the mother of this particular child, at this time in her life. The fact that women seek abortion shows us that sometimes a woman finds the vision unconscionable or sadly unworkable; then, to use Lindemann's terminology, she decides not to call this foetus into personhood.

Those who oppose abortion, and many who would like to see fewer abortions, presume that women are deliberately not considering this life as a baby. They believe that encouraging a woman to see the foetus as a baby will reduce the likelihood of her terminating the pregnancy. They appear to underestimate the woman's deliberations on her circumstances. Images of an early-stage foetus are made to look as 'baby'-like as possible. Women are encouraged to delay their decision, to have scans, hear the heartbeat and think about the baby. Furedi writes that this may have an emotional impact on a woman but there is no evidence that it changes their mind. 'Women do not seek abortions because they are ignorant that the foetus is a potential child – they seek abortion precisely *because* they know it.'[29] The decision to terminate the pregnancy will be a complex mix of concerns for her own life and for what life would be like for the baby if this pregnancy were to progress to birth. Reader writes:

> It is striking that these deliberations by women, although of course plentiful and perennial, are by and large solitary. This must be partly because of the deeply private nature of the relationship between mother and foetus. But it is also surely at least partly because of the shame and stigma our society continues to inflict on women who 'get themselves pregnant' and realize they may not want to continue, and partly because of the open season on women that the 'debate' approach to abortion encourages.[30]

## Support or adoption

Communities that oppose abortion or simply believe that there is always a better alternative may offer help and support to the woman. Financial support may be offered through pregnancy and the early years of the child. Practical support may also be offered, and the church community may extend a welcome to this family. While such support is well meaning, and may make a difference, it is unlikely to last throughout the dependent life of this child. It may be easy to pay for nappies and offer some babysitting, but the needs of a child are complex and continuing. Churches and other community groups may overestimate what they can practically do to help. The woman must consider the way her life circumstances will be permanently changed. Even with practical help, can she commit to mothering this child? How dependent will she be on the goodness of others and how sustainable will such a relationship be? An alternative to the concerns about a baby's welfare, if born into problematic circumstances, is to encourage adoption rather than abortion. Adoption is held to be a good outcome for the child, and it often can be. It also recognizes that there are women who cannot have their own children and may welcome such a baby. As mentioned in the introduction, my husband is adopted, the second child of a young unmarried woman. He was given away shortly after birth in the early 1960s. His is a happy story with loving adopting parents. There is though, for an adopted child, always a sense of being abandoned by a mother. In his case, there was also a sense of being chosen and loved by his parents. So, I acknowledge that adoption can be a positive experience for a baby.

However, it is not an easy option for the woman bearing the child. She has done all the hard work of pregnancy and labour, built up some relationship and experienced the impact that it has had on her life. Now she has to let the baby go, knowing that this is, at some level, abandonment. She may feel conflicted about the level of choice she has. She is ending her mothering responsibility while knowing that the child continues to exist. The child may at some point call her to account. She may not know how this child is being cared for. Is it happy? Is it being loved? To live through an entire pregnancy, to give birth and then to sign away the baby, is not an easy option. Reader writes: 'It has offended those with anti-choice views that women would rather abort than continue to gestate and give the baby up afterwards. ... The violations involved in unwanted pregnancy are gravely underestimated.'[31]

Some women may choose to continue a pregnancy and have the baby adopted, but to routinely suggest this as a better option than an early abortion underestimates the experience of pregnancy and giving a child away.[32] The social stigma around the idea of not looking after your own child plays a part in the cost of such a decision. Reader goes on to say that in choosing abortion, whatever the reasons, a woman 'does not relinquish responsibility for her foetus's life. Rather she exercises her maternal moral authority to complete her responsibility early'.[33] Kamitsuka writes that abortion is a 'decision not to have a being come into the world to whom one has a mothering obligation'.[34]

## How do we talk about abortion?

In thinking pastorally about abortion, it is necessary to recognize that women use maternal thinking in making abortion decisions. It is not appropriate to characterize abortion as an anti-maternal decision, even though the choice made is not to be a mother to this potential child. An unintended pregnancy poses the question of a maternal relationship, and the possibility of such a relationship will be considered even if it is quickly dismissed. What would it be for me to become the mother of this potential child, if I give myself to the making of and caring for a new human being? Can I call this person into being? This is a concrete question, and it needs to be asked fairly quickly. To commit to becoming this mother may be done joyfully, fearfully or reluctantly. She may have no choice because an alternative is not available or potentially too dangerous. She may feel that the prospect is so difficult that she will take risks, even to her own life, rather than accepting her fate. She may be fortunate enough to live in a society where safe legal abortion is available. Availing herself of this can end the pregnancy and end her maternal responsibility. That she has decided not to become the mother of a child in these circumstances is because she understands the serious level of commitment that such a relationship requires.

Her decision to end her mothering responsibility early does not mean that she is insensible to what is being lost. I will return to this in the final chapter. She may be relieved, feeling that this beginning should never have happened, yet she might regret that she is not in a place where she can commit to a new child. Chambers writes:

> When a pregnant person aborts an unplanned or unwanted pregnancy, she may not experience any regret. But if she does regret her choice, that doesn't necessarily mean she has a desire to go back in time and decide differently. ... Regret, in this case, isn't about feeling responsible for some "bad

event" that befell the fetus. Rather, it's a recognition that the fetus was a *potential* object of love, even if one chose not to make it an *actual* object of love for oneself.[35]

Life is full of decisions that shape the future and everyone can look back at endings and beginnings, some of which we may regret even if we recognize that we would make the same decision again. A woman may already be a mother; she may later in life, in a different set of circumstances, become a mother to a new child or children. She may never become a mother to a child through choice or circumstance. The issue for her is whether she can be a mother to *this* child *now*.

Women will differ in how they narrate this loss, just as they differ in how they narrate spontaneous pregnancy loss. Seeing it as the loss of a baby is not contrary to acknowledging the part played in the termination. Women who end pregnancies, like women who lose pregnancies, will find their own way of narrating what has been lost, and that needs to be respected. Early pregnancy is precarious, and this impacts how God's role in each conception is understood. The frequency of spontaneous pregnancy loss challenges the idea that each conception is God-ordained, destined to play a particular part in the world. Why would God choose to inflict loss on those who long to be mothers while placing an unwanted burden on those who do not? Recognizing that conception and early pregnancy are, like other biological processes, more random can allow genuine sympathy for those who grieve their loss and for those who face a possible pregnancy they never intended. Suggesting that it is not God who opens and shuts the womb does not negate the belief that God cares for every aspect of life, that God can comfort the grieving, and that God can recognize the messiness of human life decisions.

The abortion decision is one point in a more complex set of circumstances. There may be issues about the circumstances of the conception, the relationships the woman is involved with, the choices that she has in life. As noted above, not all sex is fully consensual; not all relationships are healthy. The previous chapter noted the work of the Reproductive Justice movement. Loretta Ross, co-founder of Sister Song, says:

> What is reproductive justice? The right to have a child, the right not to have a child, and the right to raise your children. Everyone should have that. It's not hard to explain – it's just hard as hell to achieve.[36]

Ethnicity, poverty and other intersecting factors of marginalization can reduce access to sex education, contraception, abortion, antenatal care and safe maternity care. Access to affordable childcare, housing and other resources impact on whether women can provide for a child's needs. Abortion statistics show that numbers of abortions are higher in more deprived areas: 'Across every age group in England, as deprivation increases, abortion rates increase.'[37] In Scotland the gap in termination rates between the most and least deprived areas continues to widen.[38]

Tackling issues of inequality and poverty would make a difference to the number of abortions that happen. Tackling inequality between men and women might encourage more sexual relationships marked by mutual respect, mutual pleasure and genuine consent. Good sex education can encourage younger people to make informed and responsible decisions about their sexual behaviour. The ability to communicate well with a sexual partner increases the likelihood of consent and of appropriate use of contraception. These are complex matters, and it seems that in some ways we are regressing rather than progressing. Reducing these inequalities could reduce the number of abortions. Even were that possible, there would still be women who get pregnant in circumstances where they cannot commit to mothering a child. Safe, early terminations allow them to make a responsible decision – a period of grace in which to say 'no, not now'. Recognizing that most abortions happen at this early stage should inform the way the subject is talked about. A small proportion of terminations happen later. Some of these may be about lack of access to earlier terminations due to factors of geography, healthcare provision or recognition of the pregnancy. Some will be because there is an issue with the health of the mother or the developing life. The next chapter will consider the issues around abortion and prenatal diagnoses.

## Notes

1 Ann Furedi, 2021, *The Moral Case for Abortion: A Defence of Reproductive Choice*, 2nd edn, Basingstoke: Palgrave Macmillan, p. 30.

2 UK Office for Health Improvement and Disparities, 2025, 'Abortion Statistics, England and Wales, 2022', www.gov.uk/government/statistics/abortion-statistics-for-england-and-wales-2022, accessed 01.05.2025.

3 Public Health Scotland, 2024, 'Termination of Pregnancy Statistics: Year Ending December 2023', Publichealthscotland.scot/publications/termination-of-pregnancy-statistics, accessed 01.05.2025.

4 Catriona Mackenzie, 1992, 'Abortion and Embodiment', *Australasian Journal of Philosophy* 70(2), June, pp. 136–55, https://doi.org/10.1080/00048409212345041, accessed 01.05.2025.

5 Tina Beattie, 2009, 'Catholicism, Choice and Consciousness: A Feminist Theological Perspective on Abortion', *International Journal of Public Theology* 4(1), p. 68, https://doi.org/10.1163/187251710X12578338897863, accessed 01.05.2025.

6 Ann J. Cahill, 2015, 'Miscarriage and Intercorporeality', *Journal of Social Philosophy* 46(1), March, p. 55, https://doi.org/10.1111/josp.12082, accessed 01.05.2025.

7 Helen Oppenheimer, 1992, 'Abortion: a Sketch from a Christian View', *Studies in Christian Ethics* 5(2), pp. 46–60.

8 Amy L. B. Peeler, 2022, *Women and the Gender of God*, Grand Rapids, Michigan: William B. Eerdmans Publishing Company, p. 26.

9 Soran Reader, 2008, 'Abortion, Killing, and Maternal Moral Authority', *Hypatia* 23(1), March, pp. 132–49, https://doi.org/10.1111/j.1527-2001.2008.tb01169.x, accessed 01.05.2025.

10 O'Donnell, *Dark Womb*, p. 99.

11 Furedi, *The Moral Case for Abortion*, p. 11.

12 Beattie, 'Catholicism, Choice and Consciousness'.

13 Kamitsuka, *Abortion and the Christian Tradition*.

14 'Request a Baby Loss Certificate', Gov.UK, n.d., https://www.gov.uk/request-baby-loss-certificate, accessed 01.05.2025.

15 Kate Parsons, 2010, 'Feminist Reflections on Miscarriage, in Light of Abortion', *IJFAB: International Journal of Feminist Approaches to Bioethics* 3(1), March, p. 3, https://doi.org/10.3138/ijfab.3.1.1, accessed 01.05.2025.

16 K. Lindsey Chambers, 2020, 'It's Complicated: What Our Attitudes toward Pregnancy, Abortion, and Miscarriage Tell Us about the Moral Status of Early Fetuses', *Canadian Journal of Philosophy* 50(8), November, p. 950, https://doi.org/10.1017/can.2020.48, accessed 01.05.2025.

17 Parsons, 'Feminist Reflections on Miscarriage', p. 8.

18 Parsons, 'Feminist Reflections on Miscarriage', p. 16.

19 See Kamitsuka, *Abortion and the Christian Tradition*, p. 145.

20 Hilde Lindemann, 2016, *Holding and Letting Go: The Social Practice of Personal Identities*, Oxford/New York/Auckland: Oxford University Press, p. 37.

21 Lindemann, *Holding and Letting Go*, p. 46.

22 Lindemann, *Holding and Letting Go*, p. 48.

23 Elisabeth Moltmann-Wendel, 1995, *I Am My Body: A Theology of Embodiment*, New York: Continuum, p. 15.

24 Reader, 'Abortion, Killing, and Maternal Moral Authority', p. 142.

25 Rebecca Todd Peters, 2018, *Trust Women: A Progressive Christian Argument for Reproductive Justice*, Boston: Beacon Press, p. 72.

26 David Fergusson, 2018, *The Providence of God: A Polyphonic Approach*, Current Issues in Theology, New York: Cambridge University Press, p. 335.

27 UK Office for Health Improvement and Disparities, 'Abortion Statistics'.

28 Antonia Biggs, 2013, 'Understanding Why Women Seek Abortions', *BMC Women's Health* 13(1), p. 29.

29 Furedi, *The Moral Case for Abortion*, p. 44.

30 Reader, 'Abortion, Killing, and Maternal Moral Authority', p. 142.

31 Reader, 'Abortion, Killing, and Maternal Moral Authority', p. 43.

32 Mary O'Leary Wiley and Amanda L. Baden, 2005, 'Birth Parents in Adoption: Research, Practice, and Counseling Psychology', *The Counseling Psychologist* 33(1), January, pp. 13–50, https://doi.org/10.1177/0011000004265961, accessed 01.05.2025.

33 Reader, 'Abortion, Killing, and Maternal Moral Authority', p. 143.

34 Kamitsuka, *Abortion and the Christian Tradition*, p. 131.

35 Chambers, 'It's Complicated', p. 965.

36 'Reproductive Justice', https://www.sistersong.net/reproductive-justice, accessed 01.05.2025.

37 UK Office for Health Improvement and Disparities, 'Abortion Statistics'.

38 Public Health Scotland, 'Termination of Pregnancy Statistics'.

# 4
# Prenatal Diagnosis and Abortion

This chapter will consider abortions that occur when the developing foetus is diagnosed with an anomaly. These pregnancies are, for the most part, wanted. The expectation and the plan is to have a healthy baby. Making the decision to end the pregnancy involves navigating the desire for a child and processing the concerns raised, which might mean letting go of this potential child. The fact that these pregnancy endings are called 'abortions' can be difficult for those concerned, who want to differentiate themselves from those who do not want to be pregnant. These abortion decisions do not carry the stigma of sexual licentiousness; the sex was procreative and the conception welcomed. There is no rejection of motherhood per se. They are often narrated as medical decisions. As such, they may be spoken about more openly, and women having these abortions may be offered more pastoral support and rituals to mark the loss of their baby. Surveys on public attitudes to abortion find that abortion in the case of potential disability for the child is considered more acceptable than other reasons for an abortion.[1]

However, there is concern raised about these abortions and the wide use of prenatal testing for certain conditions. Is this a form of eugenics? Disability rights activists and some disability theologians challenge the language of tragedy that narrates prenatal diagnoses. They question whether the desire for a 'perfect' child fails to recognize the diversity of humanity. They maintain that those who have different needs may also bring different rewards. Recognizing the different perspectives on life that those with disabilities can offer may be an enriching experience, a blessing for those who share life with them. Yet, the reality of caring for a child with profound needs genuinely frightens potential parents. Whether such fears can be ameliorated is part of the difficult discussion around abortion in these circumstances. It should not be judged as selfish to consider whether the personal, familial and societal support will be there to mitigate those fears.

Women wanting to have a baby in the UK, and in other countries with advanced health care, will be given advice about how to stay healthy with the expectation that in doing so, they can ensure a healthy child at the end of pregnancy. They will be encouraged to check any medications and to avoid alcohol, recreational drugs, cigarettes, unpasteurized cheese and other foods deemed risky. Taking folic acid is recommended to reduce the risk of spina bifida.[2] Keeping an eye on weight gain, attending prenatal check-ups and generally looking after their health is all encouraged. Yet, none of these actions can guarantee a healthy pregnancy. As noted in the last chapter, a significant proportion of pregnancies will end early through spontaneous miscarriages. It is assumed that many of these are due to developmental abnormalities. Developmental problems can also lead to later pregnancy loss or a stillbirth. Some developmental or chromosomal issues will be obvious at birth, while others will only be diagnosed in the early years. When all the expectation has been for a healthy baby, it can be extremely hard to discover that their child's life will be different from the one imagined.

Medical and scientific advances mean that there is a greater understanding of why some babies are born with certain conditions that may be considered disabling. Drugs, both medical and recreational, cross the placenta and can affect the development of the foetus, causing different levels of disability. Infections caught in pregnancy can also have lasting effects. Other factors, such as the woman's age and aspects of her health, can impact the genetic material held in the ovum and/or the development in the womb. Similar factors may also affect the sperm and the genetic material it brings to the embryo. Sometimes both parents carry a gene mutation that does not affect them but which, if inherited from both, will be expressed in the baby. Other chromosomal or developmental anomalies seem to arise randomly. There is still much that is not known or understood about the complexity of human reproduction. Even with medical improvements in obstetrics, birth can still be risky for both the mother and the child.

Ultrasound scans offer the possibility of viewing the developing life in the womb. Developmental anomalies can be observed that will severely impact the potential for life outside the womb. Screening and diagnostic testing also make it possible to indicate the probability of a genetic condition, though not the severity of such a condition. As such testing becomes more sophisticated, it is likely that more conditions will be identified before birth. The current language around prenatal testing emphasizes information and choice. The parents can be told of possible problems and then offered interventions. Where treatment of conditions is not an option, the choice is to continue the pregnancy – albeit better prepared for a baby with such a condition – or to terminate the pregnancy. As many of the diagnostic procedures take time, these decisions are often made later in pregnancy in the second trimester and will account for many of the post-20-week abortions that happen. Some of these abortions will end early a pregnancy that would have ended in loss later, through miscarriage or a stillbirth.

The longer a woman is pregnant, the more stress is placed on her body, so ending a non-viable pregnancy makes medical sense, although not necessarily emotional sense. In other cases, a decision needs to be made about the potential disabilities of a child with this condition. Can the mother or parents commit to that future or not? The diagnosis changes the expectation for the parents, as experts tell them of a child whose life will be shaped by disability. This will not be the baby they have been imagining. Parents make decisions within cultural understandings of disability; these may contain assumptions and prejudices that would not be shared by those with such conditions or those who care for them. Parents will also try to assess how well any increased caring needs will be supported.

Disability campaigners and theologians question the model of disability presented in these circumstances. It is based on a 'tragic' view of disability and a privileging of medical ideas of a normal child. In a recent Church of England General Synod (July 2024), the Ven Pete Spiers, an archdeacon in the Diocese of Liverpool, proposed a motion to affirm the human dignity of disabled children. Its first point 'challenges the common assumption that bringing a disabled child into the world is a tragedy to be avoided'.[3] The motion then called for better provision of support for those caring for children with disabilities and better counselling for those receiving a prenatal diagnosis of some 'anomaly'. Spiers stressed that this was not an anti-abortion motion; he was not criticizing those who did choose to terminate a pregnancy after a prenatal diagnosis. However, he quoted statistics to show the number of terminations following diagnosis of disability (though these were not contextualized), expressing concern at the high numbers. He voiced a widely held concern that, within the medical setting of prenatal testing, there is a presumption towards terminating a pregnancy after a foetal diagnosis. This concern is borne out by the figures, which show that 87% of positive diagnoses of Down's syndrome led to a termination.[4] The Archbishop of York and a few other bishops had made a statement in 2021 on this issue: 'There is something profoundly disturbing in our current contradictory stance which says that people living with disability are valued, respected and cherished, but that disability in and of itself represents a valid ground for abortion.'[5]

The fact that in this debate Spiers was careful not to condemn those who did terminate pregnancies in these circumstances is very interesting. This shows his awareness that many in the Church of England would view a prenatal diagnosis of disability as one of the exceptional reasons for a termination. It is also interesting that no member of synod used the debate to raise objection to abortion or to designate abortion as sinful. It tells us something about the way these abortions are viewed differently, an issue that may be troubling for a number of reasons. The focus of the debate was on valuing the disabled while also stressing the difficult choices individuals made. Pete Spiers spoke movingly of his own life story. His disability was caused by the drug thalidomide, which his mother, like so many, took in early pregnancy with no knowledge of any risk. The thalidomide scandal played a significant part in the public acceptance of legal abortion. It was followed by the rubella (German measles) epidemic in the USA in 1963. The fear of giving birth to a 'deformed child' expressed by middle-class married women transformed abortion requests from 'deviant to decent'.[6]

This chapter will examine how thalidomide and rubella changed attitudes to abortion. It will then explore the current standard prenatal tests that are offered and the potential of future testing. Many prenatal diagnoses indicate a disorder that has a spectrum of symptoms, and it will not be clear to what extent the given baby will manifest the condition. Parents are consistently reminded that it is for them to make the decisions, yet they need to do so in time-pressured situations often with uncertainty about what the diagnosis predicts. The developing discipline of disability theology seeks to offer a non-tragic view of the disabled child and is part of a growing change in the language used to speak about differences in human bodies and abilities, challenging ideas of 'normal'.

However, the realities of caring for a child with serious disabilities cannot be denied. Even in societies where there is state support, the birth of a child with disabilities may well require significant life changes for the parents and any other family members. Research in some cases has helped to find ways of preventing some developmental disorders in the womb. If prevention is a positive way of preventing certain conditions, is screening and abortion also a responsible way of doing the same thing?

## Thalidomide and rubella changing public opinion

The thalidomide scandal shocked the world in the early 1960s. Pictures of babies born without limbs were widely shared in the media. Far more serious disabilities that many babies were born with were hinted at; doctors, midwives and parents were deeply shocked at the birth of 'monster' babies.[7] In 1961, an Australian obstetrician and midwife made the connection between the drug thalidomide and these very unusual 'birth defects'. The drug was licensed in 46 countries as a mild sedative to help with insomnia, morning sickness and anxiety in pregnancy. It was also part of a flu medication. More than 10,000 babies were born with a range of severe deformities; about 40% of these died shortly after birth. The drug was also connected to a significant rise in miscarriages.

Research later discovered that the drug affected the early development of the embryo/foetus. The day of gestation on which the drug was taken led to specific areas of the body developing abnormally; this accounted for the range of developmental anomalies from central brain damage to missing limbs. If taken later in pregnancy, the drug would not affect the development of the baby at all. In the UK, thalidomide was licensed in 1958 and withdrawn in 1962. During this period, approximately 2,000 babies were born with birth defects and about half of them died within a few months. In 2011, 450 thalidomide survivors were recorded in the UK. The drug was not licensed in the USA, as the FDA required further assurances unconnected to developmental anomalies. However, the images of thalidomide babies were widely circulated and discussed in the USA. The language around these images was dehumanizing and frightening, with the babies being labelled 'deformed' and 'abnormal'.

When knowledge of the drug's effect became known, women who were pregnant and knew that they had taken the drug considered abortion rather than having a baby damaged by thalidomide. However, abortion was not a legal option. It is not clear how many women accessed private or back-street abortions. In the USA, there was a possibility of a 'therapeutic abortion', which in some states could be granted by a special panel. The experience of Sherri Finkbine, a children's TV presenter, raised the issue across the media. She had knowingly taken thalidomide, brought back from Europe by her husband to help with sickness in her fifth pregnancy. Reflecting on the impact a severely disabled child would have on the life of her four children, she requested a therapeutic abortion. She is quoted as saying: 'If I have no choice I would have the baby. But I have the way to prevent this tragedy, this sadness.' She spoke of her concern for her family and her belief that God had offered her 'the power to prevent' the birth of a 'malformed baby'.[8] The Arizona state panel refused her request. She chose to travel to Sweden where she had a termination; the foetus was severely affected by thalidomide. Her experience was widely covered by the media, using her story to argue that abortion was the responsible choice of a married woman who cared for her four children, even though it was not a legal option in her own country.

In a Gallup poll at the time, 52% of Americans believed that she had 'done the right thing'. The debate was also happening in the UK. The Abortion Law Reform Association (ALRA) shared a cartoon, first published in *Private Eye*, referring to thalidomide. A doctor says to a young woman: 'Young lady, I gave you a perfectly legal prescription, but you are asking me for an illegal operation.'[9] Shocked by the impact of this drug on the developing foetus, support for legal abortion increased. An opinion poll carried out in the UK in July 1962 showed 72% support for legal abortion if there was reason to suspect that the foetus was 'deformed' (as the language used put it).[10]

As the thalidomide scandal broke, Europe and the United States were being warned about an epidemic of rubella, commonly known as German measles. In the 1940s, a link had been made between rubella in early pregnancy and certain birth defects. With the concerns of thalidomide in the public mind, the epidemic predicted that more women were at risk of delivering babies with serious disabilities. Unlike thalidomide, which women could avoid taking, avoiding exposure to the disease was far from easy. As a mild but highly contagious disease, rubella was most often passed from children to their mothers. Mothers were encouraged to isolate themselves for the early months of pregnancy, but few would be able to do so. In the USA, experts predicted that 20,000 'damaged babies' would be born. Women exposed to the disease were told they had a 50% chance of having a 'deformed child'.

Reagan writes that in the USA, thalidomide woke people up: 'as women learned of rubella's effects on pregnancy, many avidly sought abortions from doctors.'[11] They asked doctors for 'therapeutic abortions', abortions that could be legally justified for the sake of the pregnant woman's health. In fact, they were being sought, and often given, to prevent the birth of a severely disabled child. *Life* magazine on 4 June 1965 covered the story of two women having abortions in a hospital setting because of their exposure to German measles. One of the mothers declared that she was a Catholic and implied that she had found a sympathetic hearing from a priest.[12] This sparked correspondence in which the Catholic Church reiterated that abortion was a sin and murder, while Protestant clergy and Jewish rabbis declared that in some circumstances, it may be permissible.

The thalidomide scandal and rubella epidemic raised the question of whether the risk of a disabled child was grounds to terminate the pregnancy. In both cases, the language of tragedy was used to describe affected babies. Many of those born after exposure to the drug or disease were expected to be institutionalized. 'Parents of children born with malformations saw a lonely, outcast and dependent future written on the bodies of their children.'[13] In her history of the rubella epidemic in the USA in 1963–5, Reagan describes how white, middle-class married women were depicted making the difficult decision to terminate their pregnancy after being exposed to rubella. Many doctors accepted that the potential of a severely disabled child because of rubella was justification for a therapeutic abortion. She concludes:

German measles together with thalidomide produced a new image of abortion as respectable and a need of married middle-class white women ... the representation of abortion was changed from a shameful thoughtless and sick action to an ethical and responsible one.[14]

This was abortion on the advice of medics, but it was still difficult to access. In both the UK and the USA, the thalidomide scandal and rubella epidemic would play a significant part in changing attitudes towards legalized abortion. For the children who were born with disabilities and survived, many new medical procedures were developed. Prosthetics for children, paediatric surgery in cardiology, ophthalmology and other areas of need all improved with the aim of helping these children. Parents learned to adapt and campaign, or they placed children in institutions.

The impact of thalidomide on the developing foetus led to improved drug-testing regimes and encouraged women to think carefully about what they took while pregnant. A vaccine was developed for rubella. This led to a novel campaign encouraging the vaccination of children, not for their own protection, as the disease is very mild, but to protect the unborn. The campaign in the USA used comics and stories to convince children of the risks of not being vaccinated and so inadvertently causing a tragedy. Reagan writes: 'Health education materials not only taught the public about disease and vaccines; they also taught the public about disability.'[15] The implication was that rubella babies were undesirable, and if children and parents followed the medical advice, instead of tragic births, 'normal' babies would be born. With little support, the impact of a disabled child on a family was then, and still can be, immense. One mother describing the impact of a disabled child on her other children writes: 'If serious disorders cannot be prevented or cured, then we must surely allow parents to detect and eliminate – or should I say spare? – those afflicted innocents for whom the normal patterns of life are forever out of reach.'[16]

Yet, the desire to prevent the birth of children with disabilities can impact on how those who are born are spoken about.

## HOW DO WE TALK ABOUT ABORTION?

In its 1965 report, the Church of England raised concerns about the use of abortion as a response to detected disability in the embryo or foetus. The report highlighted that it could reflect poorly on how people living with disability were valued.[17] However, although this report was taken seriously by those who drew up the legislation, when the 1967 Abortion Act was passed, it did allow abortion on the grounds of foetal disability. It stated as one of the permitted grounds for abortion: 'That there is a substantial risk that if the child were born it would suffer from such physical or mental abnormalities as to be seriously handicapped.' This remains the case in UK law, and while the legal limit for abortion has been lowered to 24 weeks, abortion on the grounds of foetal disability is allowed, on medical advice, up to the point of birth. Statistically, few abortions happen at this late stage, and the question of whether to change the law was the subject of a parliamentary report in 2013, which, while not recommending a change, made many recommendations to improve the way that the subject of screening, prenatal diagnosis and the option to terminate or not are handled. It was noted by one of those on the panel that 'an exclusively medical model of disability' was being used.[18]

Initial attempts to legalize abortion in parts of the USA on the grounds of foetal abnormality were proposed in response to thalidomide and rubella. The Humane Abortion Act proposed in California in 1965 aimed to protect mothers, families and children by allowing therapeutic abortions for suspected foetal disability. The proposed law was strongly opposed by the Roman Catholic Church with well-organized preaching, letter-writing and campaigns that used increasingly brutal language about abortion. It was 'lynching in the womb', Reagan writes. 'Individual women, thinking hard about their families and their own lives from different religious viewpoints, were equated with murderous mobs and genocidal dictators.'[19] She notes that there was religious support for the law from Episcopalians, Methodists and other Protestant Churches as well as Jewish groups. More than 1,000 clergy and rabbis wrote in support of lifting the 'evil' restrictions of the abortion laws 'that prevented doctors caring for their patients and prohibited women from making moral choices about their pregnancy and childbearing'.[20] The eventual law passed in California did little to permit abortion and removed foetal abnormality as a ground for a therapeutic abortion. In the Roe vs Wade ruling of 1973, abortion was legalized across the USA as a private decision. The recent reversal in 2022 has meant different states can pass their own laws restricting access to abortion, and where it is restricted, foetal abnormality is not usually an allowable exception.

In reflecting on this history, it is interesting to note that the discussion around access to abortion was changed by the fear of having a disabled child after exposure to a drug or disease. Abortion was being discussed without concerns of immoral sexual behaviour. Women challenged the expectation that they must continue a pregnancy knowing they were at risk of having a child with serious disabilities. It was reasoned that the risk alone should be grounds for ending a pregnancy. The language of therapeutic or medical abortion was used to differentiate this from an abortion for an unwanted pregnancy. The majority of these women were married, many already mothers, so they were deemed socially respectable and not seen as being anti-motherhood. Some of them even narrated abortion, like other medical procedures, as part of God's provision of medical knowledge to improve life outcomes.

## Prenatal diagnosis and screening

The women who worried about thalidomide and rubella were conscious of their exposure but uncertain of the impact on the pregnancy. There was no way of knowing how badly their baby might have been affected, the chance of survival and the future of the life they might lead. The fear that meant women wanted an abortion was based on the worst-case scenario. Advances in medical technology and genetics mean that some developmental 'anomalies' can now be observed during pregnancy.

Risk factors for certain conditions can be calculated through screening and further diagnostic tests offered. Pregnant women are asked to make time-sensitive decisions about whether to have tests and how to respond to risk factors. When diagnoses are made, they will be asked whether they wish to terminate the pregnancy or continue preparing for the future of a child that may have increased care needs. Again, women are usually concerned about worst-case scenarios, wondering how they, their families and the child will cope. They find themselves in a medical and scientific world trying to make family decisions. Rayna Rapp, reflecting on these choices, writes that a prenatal diagnosis 'forces each woman to act as a moral philosopher of the limits, adjudicating the standards guarding entry into the human community for which she serves as normalizing gatekeeper'.[21]

In the UK, antenatal care is provided by the NHS, and the options of testing for foetal anomalies are outlined as standard offerings that can be chosen or refused. However, the routine scans offered are part of this diagnostic process, offering the chance to 'see' the baby and take home pictures; this has all become an expected part of the pregnancy experience, and it can be hard to turn these down. Thus, even if people choose not to take the blood screening offered, most will want the scans, even though they might be diagnostic. The framing of prenatal tests suggest that it is good to know how the baby is developing. Women may well be using pregnancy books or apps that show them weekly 'updates' on the baby's development. These are, of course, generic and merely show an average pregnancy. Knowing that the baby is conforming to 'normal' development can reassure that all is well. Most women will be reassured. For some, however, a condition will be diagnosed that can be treated either in the womb or shortly after birth. For others, the scans will show developmental problems that mean there is no possibility of life outside the womb, or that the baby will die shortly after birth. Alternatively, it can show that this baby is developing differently, not in a life-threatening way but in ways that will significantly impact its life beyond the womb.

Pregnant women in the UK are offered a scan at 10–14 weeks; one of the main aims of this is to date the pregnancy. However, certain developmental conditions such as spina bifida may be identified at this stage. If the mother has agreed to testing for Down's syndrome, Patau syndrome and Edward Turner syndrome, all resulting from a specific third chromosome, then the nuchal translucency will be measured – that is, the fluid at the back of the foetal neck. The result of this measurement will be combined with the maternal age and the results of a blood-screening test, to calculate a risk factor for this pregnancy. If the risk is high, then invasive tests may be offered to diagnose the condition. Chorionic villus sampling (CVS) removes fluid from the placenta and can be carried out at 11–14 weeks of pregnancy. Amniocentesis removes fluid from the amniotic sac and can be carried out at 15–20 weeks of pregnancy. Both carry a risk of miscarriage, though improved techniques have reduced this risk to slight, but not negligible. A second ultrasound scan is offered at about 20 weeks, and this is described as 'an anomaly scan'. The NHS website states:

> The scan checks the physical development of your baby, although it cannot pick up every condition. ... It allows the sonographer to look for 11 rare conditions. ... Scans cannot find all conditions, and there's always a chance that the baby may be born with a health issue that scans could not have seen.[22]

The standard tests offered in the anomaly scan look for conditions that are identifiable either through physical observation or chromosomal sequencing. Some of what is observed may indicate that the baby will not be able to survive for long outside the womb, or that it may not survive until birth. Developmental issues with major organs that cannot be rectified by medical intervention may be clearly identifiable. The option to end a pregnancy early when it is known that there will not be a live birth is seen as a kindness, and medically better for the mother, though not all expectant mothers will take this option.

## HOW DO WE TALK ABOUT ABORTION?

Pregnancy and childbirth place stresses on a woman's body and it can be harmful to insist that a woman continues a non-viable pregnancy. In places where abortion legislation is very restrictive, women's lives have been endangered through an insistence that either the foetus must have already died in the womb or the woman be about to die herself, before an intervention is allowed. The case of Savita Halappanavar in the Republic of Ireland, where a failure to intervene for fear of breaking the law led to her death in 2012, had a significant impact on the decision to adopt a more liberal abortion law there.

Other concerns will be less clear cut. Invasive tests may show that there is a chromosomal condition such as Down's syndrome. Abortion is offered as an option for those who have a diagnosis of a 'serious' anomaly. The wording of the Abortion Act speaks of a child that if born 'would suffer from such physical or mental abnormalities as to be seriously handicapped'. This language is dated, and it is not clear exactly what it means. It is, to some extent, subjective, particularly utilizing the concept of suffering. Is the concern for the wellbeing of the child? Families with a history of a genetic condition may seek bespoke screening for conditions that have affected previous children or family members. In that case, they will have an informed view of what is involved in terms of both potential suffering and care needs for an affected child. Where a previous child has been cared for and loved, but suffered and died in infancy, it is understandable that parents will want to know if a subsequent pregnancy is going to lead to the same diagnosis. They may feel that they cannot go through a similar experience of grief and loss.

In most cases, parents have little or no experience of the condition the foetus has been diagnosed with. They can only draw on knowledge they have from wider society to imagine life with an affected child. Information about the most frequently diagnosed conditions is offered with links to organizations that support and advocate. Such organizations can offer advice and parental stories. They may also seek to change the perception of the diagnosis from a 'tragedy' to the possibility of an enriched life caring for someone who is different. The theological ethicist Brian Brock, whose work we will look at later, suggests that instead of tragedy, there needs to be an attitude of wonder: 'A genetically anomalous child can be experienced not as "negative pregnancy outcome" synonymous with misfortune, but as joyous and enlightening liberation.'[23]

Those who feel unable, unwilling or under-resourced to take on the responsibility of this potential child may choose to terminate a pregnancy after a diagnosis. They may be offered a surgical abortion, performed under anaesthetic, to remove the pregnancy. This is usually only offered in NHS hospitals before 13 weeks of pregnancy, although it can be accessed through other abortion providers before 24 weeks of pregnancy. Such an operation will damage the foetus, meaning that there is no possibility of a body to see or hold. The alternative is a medically induced abortion, which will involve, if early in pregnancy, an induced miscarriage or, if later, labouring to deliver the dead baby. In later terminations, an injection to the foetus will ensure that it has died before labour begins. The mother and those supporting her may wish to hold the dead baby if it has reached a stage where that is possible. They may well experience the loss as they would a miscarriage or stillbirth. The abortions that happen after foetal diagnoses are usually sensitively managed. They tend to be differentiated from 'other' abortions. One leaflet given to those who are terminating a pregnancy because of foetal anomalies recognizes the stress that might be experienced in being 'in an environment where most terminations are happening because the pregnancy is unwanted'.[24] In Rapp's study of women terminating after a foetal diagnosis, she comments on this. She found women distinguish between 'good mothers in bad situations' and 'girls unfit to be mothers', between 'good aborters' and 'bad aborters'. She writes: 'I was forced to recognize the *cultural judgements* that many women with a positive diagnosis make about their own circumstances: They consider themselves to be appropriate mothers, and therefore, tragically, appropriate aborters.'[25]

## Don't screen us out

The assumption that abortions after a foetal diagnosis are more acceptable than those where the pregnancy is unplanned is reinforced by the idea that these are medical decisions aiming to prevent 'unhealthy' babies from being born. This raises the question of whose suffering is driving the decision-making. Is the issue the future suffering of the child, or the suffering of parents and wider family members? Is there also a social resource issue? Children and adults with complex needs may require more state-funded support. Currently, the genetic conditions tested for are limited by the procedures that are available. The recent development of non-invasive prenatal testing (NIPT) means that genome-wide foetal profiling may soon be available early in pregnancy. It has been introduced in a number of hospitals and provides more accurate indication of a potential Down's diagnosis. This test can be used earlier in pregnancy and can potentially diagnose a greater number of congenital and hereditable anomalies with more accuracy. This raises the question of who should decide what is screened for and whether such decisions run the risk of 'structural directivity'. In other words, who decides what conditions count as a serious level of suffering?

Alongside this question is the concern that decisions to terminate may be made for less 'serious' issues. The question of sex selection for cultural or familial reasons is often raised. The European Society of Human Genetics (ESHG) and American Society of Human Genetics (ASHG) note a concern about the 'trivialization' of abortion if prenatal testing leads to couples using abortion 'for unimportant (that is, not for avoiding suffering) or for discriminatory reasons'.[26] Yet, as Stapleton maintains, this already presumes that there is agreement about what is important and what is discriminatory. He suggests that the screening currently offered can already be characterized as discriminatory, prejudicing certain conditions. He also notes that the reasons why certain non-medical conditions might factor in individual abortion decisions may, if taken in context, not be 'trivial'.[27] The medical professionals involved maintain that they mitigate discriminatory advice by ensuring that the decision to test and to act on any diagnosis is an informed choice made by the mother. There is a presumption that neutrality can be maintained by the medical team involved.

Testing is optional, and at each stage of the process it is the mother's decision how to proceed – in consultation with her partner, if appropriate. Health workers should be non-directive. Stapleton comments on the guidelines promoted in the UK, Netherlands and other Western countries:

> The two most characteristic features of this framework are that health services should adopt a position of neutrality with respect to the outcomes of couples' reproductive choices (i.e. there are no preferred pre- or post-test choices) and should support couples in making informed and autonomous reproductive choices in line with their own values of whether or not to have an affected child.[28]

Yet, these decisions must be made within a limited time frame with whatever information is available. A woman must let go of the imagined child and reimagine a different scenario. She will do this alongside those who will share in the life and care of a future child. She will do so within a familial, societal and cultural framework about disability and different types of disability. She now knows things that she did not know and will be treated as someone with a problematic pregnancy.

Disability rights movements and disability theology aim to challenge medical and societal models of humanity that devalue lives that do not conform to a perceived 'normality'. To talk about anomalies in foetal development, it is claimed, perpetuates a biomedical understanding that cannot see that such differences may be a valuable part of human existence, in all its complex diversity. Those who advocate as people with Down's syndrome and those who know, love and care for them want to tell their stories about fulfilling lives and joyful families. They maintain that the very fact of screening for Down's syndrome gives a negative message about people with that chromosomal make-up. The campaign 'Don't Screen Us Out' is organized by people with Down's syndrome, their families and carers. As mentioned at the start of this chapter, almost 90% of pregnancies with a diagnosis of Down's syndrome are terminated in the UK. They suggest that this is eugenics: that is systematically trying to eradicate people with Down's syndrome based on outdated and prejudicial ideas. They also challenge the fact that testing for Down's is offered with termination as an option in the UK beyond the agreed point of viability, in fact up until birth.

While it is not known what leads to the extra chromosome present in Down's syndrome and other trisomy conditions, it is known that maternal age is a significant risk factor. In many parts of the world, and certainly in the UK, average maternal age is rising, leading to a rise in the numbers of foetuses diagnosed with the syndrome. Currently, there is no preventative measure apart from discouraging older women from pregnancy, which seems socially unacceptable and may also be unpredictable. In my own experience of contemplating a third child in my late thirties, the risks of conceiving a child with Down's was one of the factors that made me decide not to have any more children. I was a parish priest and within the congregation we had an adult with Down's syndrome, whose parents I also knew well. I had offered pastoral support to parents who had given birth to a baby diagnosed as having Down's syndrome and to parents who had terminated a pregnancy after a diagnosis. I had also seen the grief of a woman who miscarried after an amniocentesis, the foetus showing no signs of any anomalies. The question whether to test had become complex for me. In earlier pregnancies, it had seemed straightforward not to have any testing and to commit to what would be. However, now I was unsure, not least because I would be making a potential decision that would impact on my two children.

Medical knowledge of pregnancy and foetal development continues to advance. Yet, there is still so much that is not known. The high number of early pregnancies that end in miscarriage shows the complexity of early development, with the assumption that abnormal development is probably responsible for many early foetal deaths and subsequent miscarriages. The development of embryos outside the womb for fertility treatment involves screening to ensure that the healthiest embryos are implanted, recognizing that some already show developmental abnormalities at this early stage. Research has identified ways of preventing some of these developmental anomalies. Good levels of folic acid in early pregnancy reduces the development of spina bifida, and this has led not just to advice for women to take supplements if planning a pregnancy, but also to the enriching of flour and cereals in many countries with folic acid to dose potentially pregnant women. As noted earlier, women are encouraged to modify what they eat and drink, and what medication they take during pregnancy. They are also encouraged to think about their weight, as the mother's obesity raises the risk of certain developmental anomalies. I am aware that prevention is seen differently from termination, yet the aim of prevention is to reduce or stop the prevalence of certain conditions, effectively screening them out. There are disorders and diseases that have been wiped out or considerably limited. If a supplement or medication was found to prevent chromosomal trisomy, then it is likely that women would be encouraged to take it. If, like folic acid, it could be included in widely eaten food, then they might have no choice. Is this screening out, or is the problem that prevention is only considered reasonable before conception? I note that Sherri Finkbine, mentioned earlier in this chapter, saw her abortion of a thalidomide baby as God's offer of prevention.

The issue of what can be diagnosed and how decisions are made is only going to get more complicated. Stapleton writes:

> as the scope of screening expands the amount of information that each couple must process is likely to increase. The central ethical issue here is the risk of uninformed reproductive choice ... Yet ... limiting the scope of screening in order to reduce the risk of informational overload may also increase its structural directivity.[29]

Already the decisions that need to be made in a short time frame can be overwhelming. Heather Renée Morgan writes that parents have to let go of what they 'know' to be true – that is, their expectation that all is progressing well and the baby they will birth in due course will be considered healthy. After the diagnosis of a condition or heightened risk factor, 'Parents-to-be may face new waves of epistemic unravelling ... as they come to realize the limits of medical science, as to what can and cannot be known with certainty, and what may or may not be "fixable", are revealed.'[30] There are people to talk to, information to be processed and a whole new future imagined. Those involved in their care aim to offer neutral advice, yet that is not easy. The fact that this is medical information plays a part in how it is received. The earlier the diagnosis, the more time there is to make a decision. The earlier the diagnosis, the less time the potential mother has had to know this life in her womb, which may make it easier to let it go.

## Wonder or tragedy?

In the opening of this chapter, I mentioned the debate in the General Synod of the Church of England in July 2024, where one motion challenged the common assumption that bringing a disabled child into the world is a tragedy to be avoided. The theological ethicist Brian Brock suggests that instead of tragedy, there needs to be an attitude of wonder. In doing so, he uses the imagery of the Annunciation: 'the annunciative call can emerge from a grainy imagery and the stony silence of a disappointed sonographer.' The calling is to see differently, to recognize that in this potential child, God is 'inviting secular humanity to attend anew to the strange ways of God's working'.[31] Shaped by the experiences of parenting his own son Adam, whose story he shares, Brock critiques a highly medicalized understanding of disability and the part that pre-natal screening plays in perpetuating a devaluing of those who are different. He draws on the work of Augustine, encouraging an attitude of wonder at God's creation. The annunciating angel told Mary to 'fear not', and Brock calls for a willingness to faithfully fear not.

The challenge is a necessary one, and yet I have a concern about moving so emphatically from tragedy to wonder and gift. Sometimes, when people are faced with fear, they can re-evaluate the situation and find the resources to move forward. Sometimes, an appropriate reaction to fear is to run away. Parents receiving a foetal diagnosis need to reimagine the life of this potential child, their own responsibilities and the family they will be in the light of a new reality. It is not helpful to be overcritical of the process of letting go of a perfectly imagined child who would fulfil their dreams and expectations, even if some aspects of such hopes may always be unrealistic. None of us can predict the future of any children we have; suggesting that we can shows a level of unreality that does need to be questioned. However, this diagnosis involves imagining pain, struggle, sacrifice, battles to be fought and responsibilities to be carried that will most likely be very different from what they had been expecting. Increasingly, couples will have thought deeply about when to have children, how they will manage and what they will bring to their life. To be fearful of the unknown is a reasonable response; to be sad about what will not be is not selfish.

If a baby or child were in an accident or suffered an illness that radically changed their abilities and the family's caring responsibilities, it would not seem inappropriate to tell them that this was a tragedy. A theodicy that suggests that God had caused or allowed such an accident or illness is deeply problematic. So too is a theodicy that says that God is at the root of this diagnosed condition. To see the diagnosis as a tragedy does not necessarily mean that the child will not be valued. Those who continue with the pregnancy may well find strength and courage, embracing a child who will change their perspectives and enable them to wonder. There are remarkable stories of how individuals and families have coped when they feared they might not. Experiencing a sense of tragedy, confusion, grief and even anger at the news that this child will be disabled does not preclude reflecting lovingly on its future. Good information can help allay fears, yet it will take time to accept this news.

Moving too quickly away from any notion of tragedy diminishes the experience of parents facing a prenatal diagnosis of an anomaly. However, acknowledging that does not preclude recognizing that those who are born with difference, even profoundly challenging conditions, can be liberating gifts. Families do speak of all that they have learned and the joy and wonder their children have brought into their lives. It is important to recognize the humanity and value of disabled children and to address how best families may be helped to care for them. The concern Brock and others raise – that the presumption of abortion as a reasonable response to a diagnosis of a disabled child may undermine how we value such people – is legitimate. He notes that this is 'obvious when the marked imbalance between investments in genetic research and technologies is compared with the resources devoted to supporting the living disability community'.[32] As noted in Stapleton's article, there is a wider question about whether the desire for prenatal screening is in part motivated by concerns about the cost burden to society.[33] Yet, quoting Kamitsuka: 'A birthing mandate is neither a practical nor an ethical way of rooting out the stigma in societal attitudes on disability.'[34]

While it is essential to value those whose lives are different and to challenge negative stereotypes, care needs to be taken in speaking about God's role in gifting a child with a condition that may be hard to bear. Kamitsuka writes that 'theology should hesitate before suggesting, even poetically, that a disabled person, or the discovery of a disability through prenatal testing, serves to announce God's will'.[35] As noted in the last chapter, it is not helpful to suggest God's involvement at the level of each conception when we know that some babies will never be born and some will be born into a life of pain and struggle. Many foetuses with congenital anomalies miscarry; it is hard to see this as God's will. There is a danger that the limitations of a medical model that explains the risk factors and randomness of developmental differences is replaced by an inscrutable God 'gifting' an unasked-for challenge in this pregnancy.

The important point is that the abortion decision is not necessarily about the intrinsic value of a child. It is about whether a woman has the capacity to commit herself to gestating this child and caring for it in the years to come. In this way, it is like any abortion decision. What might have seemed possible and even welcome if the potential child did not have complex needs may look very different in the light of a diagnosis. So much will depend on the support networks around the mother, the attitudes of those whom she will need to share in the caring. Practical and financial issues will also be considered. It is certainly true that fear of the unknown may be heightened by ignorance of children and adults with a particular condition. Good information about the joys as well as the struggles needs to be available. Yet, this is a decision made in a particular context. Rapp's study of women undergoing amniocentesis in New York showed that different communities had differing concerns about disability, some more focused on cognitive ability and some on physical appearance.[36]

## Care is gendered

Brock's use of the Annunciation story can suggest that to say 'no' to the calling of this nascent life is a failure to welcome God's gift, even to resist the Holy Spirit. However, there is a danger of equating a 'yes' to God with self-sacrifice, as if the sacrifice becomes the sign of faith. Feminist theology critiques the valorizing of lives of self-sacrifice where the sacrifice has been obligatory, where there has been no freedom to embrace it because there was no possibility of refusing it. A freely given life can be fulfilling and rewarding, yet an obligatory life of self-sacrifice can be soul-destroying. This has been a particular concern for women, where presumptions of a caring nature have justified lives of care-giving that have involved self-denial in damaging ways. Care-giving is still heavily gendered in most societies, with expectations of mothers' 'innate' capacity to care idealized. When a child's care needs are more complex and burdensome, there is a strong likelihood that the mother will take on a greater proportion of the caring tasks. 'The traditional division of labour by gender makes all children, and perhaps especially, disabled children mother's work.'[37]

In her book *Motherhood and Autism*, Eilidh Campbell notes that caring for a child with disabilities is often a gendered experience, what she describes as 'a mother's burden'.[38] Idealized models of community may suggest that the burden can be shared, but these tend to be unrealistic and impractical. In taking on the responsibility of mothering, women think about the daily practicalities of caring for their child. Concerns about a capacity to care for a child factor into most abortion decisions. When a diagnosis has been received, part of the decision-making process involves trying to understand how much greater the care needs will be for this child and for how much longer. In a planned or accepted pregnancy, there will have been tentative or actual plans for the care of the newborn and ideas about caring for a developing child. The diagnosis may mean radically changing what such care will look like and who is going to be primarily engaged in giving it.

The risk of chromosomal anomalies increases with the age of the mother. Older mothers may also already have children, and possibly also caring responsibilities for older family members. Thus, their thinking will consider the impact on siblings, both growing up and after the parents have died if they become responsible for a sibling in need of care. Where older women are having their first child, then the issue of who might take responsibility for a future adult with needs can also affect decision-making. The support networks around this mother and wider family will impact how she imagines the caring needs to be met. Campaigning for better support for those with disabilities and for those who care for them is needed. Yet, such support even when available can only do so much. Campbell comments on ideas of communal support:

While it would be tempting to imagine a community in which our responsibilities and burdens were shared and supported equally, without judgement or expectation, in reality this is a thoroughly impractical if not impossible, undertaking. It is often unfeasible for others to provide the kind of practical day-to-day support that mothers of children on the spectrum could genuinely benefit from.[39]

Abortion decisions are made in the real world, where prospective parents recognize or fear what will and will not be offered to help them care for the child. Some will find that they can embrace this difference and draw on whatever resources they can to mother this child. Good information that suggests positive stories are important to counter the narrative of tragedy, but not if they fail to acknowledge the hard work and sacrifices that are likely to be necessary.

Abortion decisions are made in context. The very concerns that Brock raises about the limited resources available to support the living disabled factor into the thinking and decision-making. The *annunciation*, the calling, to care for a life that will unfold differently, may involve considerably higher dependency for much longer than envisioned, alongside engagement with medical, social and specialist teams and a radical rethinking of family life. In the UK, the NHS provides medical care, free at the point of need, and there are statutory provisions of support for the disabled. Yet, the reality is that these are all resource-poor, and families find that much of the burden of care will be theirs. In other countries, provisions may be even more limited. While writing this book in July 2024, two news stories appeared in the UK press, each reflecting the lack of support felt by mothers in caring for children with special needs. In the first story, a mother in Northern Ireland left her disabled teenage son at his school because she could no longer cope with caring for him. The respite care that used to enable her some rest was no longer forthcoming, and she felt her only option was not to collect him from school. He was taken into full-time institutional care.[40] Far more tragically, in Salford, a mother who was recognized as deeply caring, dedicating her life to her daughter's complex needs, killed her daughter and then committed suicide. She had decided that both were better off out of this world's suffering.[41] These are extreme stories, but they need to be recognized alongside the more hopeful accounts. They bring into sharp focus the wider issue of how society supports those who seek to care lovingly in difficult circumstances.

It is true that accidents, illnesses, life happenings can plunge any family into the situation of caring for a loved one with a disability. Prenatal diagnosis can only pick up certain conditions, and some new parents will have to navigate a diagnosis and its consequences in the early days or months of their baby's life. Yet, at this stage of pregnancy, women have a choice, albeit a very difficult one. They can, and many do, end this pregnancy and embark on a subsequent pregnancy where the child is born without these complex needs. They can also end this pregnancy and decide that this is a final pregnancy, and they will focus on the children they have or on a life without children. Some women will continue to commit to the pregnancy and all its complexity because they trust that their love for this baby will sustain them through the difficulties. They will begin to consider the resources necessary for the future. Each of these women will have made a moral decision based on an assessment of her capacity to mother this child. In her study of mothers' attitudes to amniocentesis Rapp concluded:

> There is no definitive "Catholic", "Jewish", or "Protestant" position on reproductive technology, when viewed from the pregnant woman's point of view. Rather, each concrete, embedded pregnancy is assessed in light of competing claims on maternity the individual acknowledges and to which she responds.[42]

## How do we talk about abortion?

When talking about abortion, women facing a prenatal diagnosis need to be kept in mind. Many of them will be uncomfortable with the word 'abortion', associating the term with those who do not want a baby, who may even be feckless. However, it is important not to be drawn into unhelpful binaries. Distinguishing abortions in response to a prenatal diagnosis from abortions made in other circumstances may seem to be pastorally sensitive, yet I do not think it helps in thinking about abortion generally. I recognize that women in these circumstances would like different terminology, or at least a way of differentiating their action from someone who did not want to be pregnant. There can be a desire to self-identify or to be identified as 'good aborters' in contrast to those 'bad aborters' who never intended to have a child, who may well have been 'sexually incontinent'.[43] This kind of binary is implicit in exceptionalist views of abortion, such as the Church of England's stated position:

> The Church of England combines principled opposition to abortion with a recognition that there can be strictly limited conditions under which it may be morally preferable to any available alternative.[44]

This position presumes that some abortion decisions can be judged as morally reasonable, yet, by implication, that most are not.

In these cases, women are likely to see their abortions as exceptional; they have made an appropriate medically sanctioned decision. However, it is also clear that for many, the medical advice was not so clear cut. The information received predicted possibilities across a spectrum for a future child. It is not clear how complex such a child's needs would be and how much they would impact on daily life. Decisions are subjective and contextual, based on probabilities and worst-case scenarios. Someone else may respond to a similar diagnosis differently.

This makes it hard to claim any kind of certainty about a right response to a diagnosis or to delineate what the 'limited conditions' are that make this abortion 'morally preferable' to continuing the pregnancy. In these decisions, as in so many maternal decisions, it is only possible to do what seems best for all those involved. The language of exceptionalism links to the language of tragedy concerning the diagnosis, as the decision needs to be justified as morally preferable to the alternative. In fact, these abortion decisions are more morally complex than decisions to terminate an unintended pregnancy because of the impact such terminations may have on how people living with these conditions are viewed.

For many of the women ending a wanted pregnancy after a diagnosis of developmental or chromosomal anomaly, this pregnancy loss will be grieved in the same way as a miscarriage or stillbirth. Depending on the stage of gestation, they may well have shared their news of pregnancy and expectations of a baby with others, who will need to be told of their loss. For some, the narration is sad but straightforward; the diagnosis has shown that there is no possibility of life outside the womb, or the baby will die shortly after birth. For others, it is more complex as the prognosis is of a baby who will live but be affected by developmental or chromosomal anomalies. Where the public narrative of Christian attitudes to abortion ranges from total opposition to principled opposition with exceptions, it can be hard to know how the faith community will respond. This can be especially difficult when the faith community has members with different levels of disability and the decision not to have this child might be interpreted as devaluing children and adults with similar conditions. As will be further discussed in the next chapter, women think carefully about who they talk to about their abortion experience, even in these circumstances.

At the start of this chapter, it was shown how the thalidomide scandal and the German measles epidemic in the 1960s changed attitudes towards abortion. It was considered by many as not simply acceptable, but in fact responsible, to seek to terminate a pregnancy at risk from the negative effects of a drug or disease. Abortion in these cases was narrated as preventing the birth of children with potentially serious disabilities. Since the 1960s, there have been welcome changes to society's views about disability. The institutionalization of disabled children was up to then often seen as the default position; now many conditions that would have been considered life-limiting have different and better outcomes. Policies of inclusion, celebrations of disabled sports, and positive role models in mainstream media continue to alter perceptions. This means that the decisions around a prenatal diagnosis are more complex, and the language of prevention is more problematic.

Yet, it needs to be acknowledged that the development of prenatal screening and testing, followed by legal abortion, is about prevention. For some, that is how it is experienced. The earlier the diagnosis comes in the pregnancy, the more possible it is for this to be seen as a prevention. A couple I knew had a first child who was diagnosed after birth with a complex chromosomal anomaly that made her short life full of medical interventions. She was deeply loved, and deeply mourned; there is no question about how her parents valued her life. They were told that both parents carried this genetic anomaly, so subsequent pregnancies were at risk of having the same condition. They opted for testing early in pregnancy. Two pregnancies were found to have the same condition, and these were aborted. Two did not, and these pregnancies resulted in two children who have thrived. These abortions were seen as preventing the birth of another child with this complex, life-limiting condition. They did not lessen the value of their first child, who continued to be remembered lovingly and grieved. Where screening is more random, it may still be seen as preventative, if it offers the option of not giving birth to a baby with a serious disability.

Disability rights campaigners and theologians, quite rightly, question the ethics of prevention, asking at what point it becomes eugenics. They focus on wider societal questions about how disability is narrated and defined. They argue that those whose needs are more complex should be properly supported, not just by those who are the immediate carers, but by wider recognition and resourcing of their needs. They fear that prenatal screening that includes the option of abortion perpetuates medical models that suggest a disabled baby is of less worth than a 'normal' baby. There is also a fear that increased knowledge of genetics and gestational development will increase the conditions that can be screened for. This would mean that more conditions are presented as an 'unhealthy' pregnancy. Some of these may be conditions with complex needs, but others, perhaps presenting less serious challenges, may still be designated as 'abnormal'. The medical response to these concerns is to emphasize the autonomy of the mother and those close to her in making the decision. Thus, women are placed in the very difficult situation of processing complex information within a short timescale. Rapp writes, 'She must make conscious the fears, fantasies, and phobias she holds about mothering a disabled child.' She notes that at the same time she must also articulate 'the ethical impact of a positive diagnosis on themselves, other family members, and the foetus, while describing the limits of how they want to live'. [45] Information about the diagnosis, as well as positive stories from those who live with the condition and those who care for them, can help inform this decision. Yet, it will be made within the prevailing societal attitudes to disability and with limited knowledge of the kinds of support that may or may not be forthcoming.

The range of what can be diagnosed in the womb is going to increase, and pregnant women, alongside partners and other family, will be asked to make moral decisions about what to test for and how to respond to the results. This needs wider conversations including in our Churches. Informed conversations about these ethical issues need to consider the possibility of abortion. Such conversations should recognize that a decision not to continue a pregnancy can be made in good faith based on a realistic assessment of the circumstances. The decision should not be presumed as selfish, nor as an inability to acknowledge the value of those who live with different kinds of disability. Each decision is specific and contextual, and should not be read to mean that someone else should make the same decision. That some people feel that they have the resources, including faith resources, to cope with a very different family future, does not mean that others will have the same support.

Christians have an important part to play in providing affirmation of those whose lives are different and who need more complex care. The work of disability theology in challenging embedded views of how the image of God is often perceived in terms of human cognitive ability and autonomy can help develop a wider, more inclusive understanding of humanity. Societal views of disability are changing, and within the UK there are both state and charitable provisions to help in bringing up a child with specific and complex needs.

Again, Churches and Christian individuals can play a part in changing attitudes and providing support. Yet, the pressures of caring for a child with such needs should not be understated. Abortion decisions are made in concrete circumstances. These women's abortion choices may be more accepted than those of the unintended pregnant women. They are more likely to receive support to grieve their loss. They may feel able to justify their decisions as an 'exceptional' circumstance avoiding the condemnatory language around most abortions. Yet, they are of a piece with other abortion decisions. These are, as stated in the last chapter, quoting Kamitsuka, decisions to end their mothering responsibility for this child early, because they do not feel able to mother this prospective child. I use the word 'decisions' because I am conscious of how the word 'choice' can imply far more flexibility than many women feel they have. Rapp quotes Doris Paul, an African-American woman in her study. '"Choices, choices". "Decisions, decisions" would be more like it. Because we are always called to crossroads and tests, they aren't things we seek, they're situations that befall us.'[46]

# HOW DO WE TALK ABOUT ABORTION?

## Notes

1 Aisha Chabdu, 2024, 'How Are Attitudes to Abortion Changing?', National Centre for Social Research (blog), 29 October, https://natcen.ac.uk/how-are-attitudes-towards-abortion-britain-changing, accessed 02.05.2025.

2 UK Research and Innovation, 2024, 'Preventing Spina Bifida', 20 February, https://www.ukri.org/who-we-are/how-we-are-doing/research-outcomes-and-impact/mrc/preventing-spina-bifida, accessed 02.05.2025.

3 'Human Dignity of Disabled Children' (Church of England General Synod, n.d.), https://www.churchofengland.org/sites/default/files/2024-06/gs-2359a-human-dignity-disabled-children.pdf, accessed 02.05.2025.

4 Don't Screen Us Out, 2024, 'Almost 90% of all babies prenatally diagnosed with Down's syndrome were screened out by abortion in 2021, according to NHS England', press release, 28 March, https://dontscreenusout.org/press-release-almost-90-of-all-babies-prenatally-diagnosed-with-downs-syndrome-were-screened-out-by-abortion-in-2021-according-to-nhs-england, accessed 02.05.2025.

5 The Church of England, 2021, 'Bishops back women's Down's Syndrome legal challenge', press release, 6 July, https://www.churchofengland.org/media/press-releases/bishops-back-womens-downs-syndrome-legal-challenge, accessed 02.05.2025.

6 Leslie J. Reagan, 2010, *Dangerous Pregnancies: Mothers, Disabilities, and Abortion in Modern America*, Berkeley: University of California Press, p. 56.

7 Reagan, *Dangerous Pregnancies*, p. 50.

8 Reagan, *Dangerous Pregnancies*, pp. 79–80.

9 Michael Kandiah and Gillian Staerck, eds, 2002, *The Abortion Act 1967*, London: Institute of Contemporary British History, p. 34.

10 Kandiah and Staerck, *The Abortion Act 1967*, p. 17.

11 Reagan, *Dangerous Pregnancies*, p. 56.

12 Reagan, *Dangerous Pregnancies*, p. 85.

13 Reagan, *Dangerous Pregnancies*, p. 17.

14 Reagan, *Dangerous Pregnancies*, p. 93.

15 Reagan, *Dangerous Pregnancies*, p. 155.

16 Quoted in Reagan, *Dangerous Pregnancies*, p.138

17 Robin Gill, 2021, 'Church of England (Anglican) Perspectives on Abortion', in Alireza Bagheri, ed., *Abortion: Global Positions and Practices, Religious and Legal Perspectives*, Cham: Springer International Publishing, p. 68.

18 Fiona Bruce (Chair), 2013, Report of the Parliamentary Inquiry into Abortion on the Grounds of Disability, https://dontscreenusout.org/wp-content/uploads/2016/02/Abortion-and-Disability-Report-17-7-13.pdf, accessed 02.05.2025.

19 Reagan, *Dangerous Pregnancies*, p. 138.
20 Reagan, *Dangerous Pregnancies*, p. 134.
21 Rayna Rapp, 1999, *Testing Women, Testing the Fetus: The Social Impact of Amniocentesis in America*, The Anthropology of Everyday Life, New York: Routledge, p. 131.
22 NHS website, 'Ultrasound scans in pregnancy', www.nhs.uk/pregnancy/your-pregnancy-care/ultrasound-scans, accessed 02.05.2025.
23 Brian Brock, 2020, *Wondrously Wounded: Theology, Disability, and the Body of Christ*, SRTD: Studies in Religion, Theology, and Disability, Waco, Texas: Baylor University Press.
24 Antenatal Results and Choices, https://www.arc-uk.org, accessed 02.05.2025.
25 Rapp, *Testing Women, Testing the Fetus*, p. 236.
26 Quoted in Stapleton, 'Qualifying Choice'.
27 Stapleton, 'Qualifying Choice', p. 201.
28 Stapleton, 'Qualifying Choice', p. 198.
29 Stapleton, 'Qualifying Choice', p. 200.
30 Heather Renée Morgan, 2024, 'Groaning Withness: A Theological Response to Adverse Prenatal Diagnosis', in Karen O'Donnell and Claire Williams, *Pregnancy and Birth: Critical Theological Conceptions*, London: SCM Press, pp. 317–18.
31 Brock, *Wondrously Wounded*, pp. 94–5.
32 Brock, *Wondrously Wounded*, p. 81.
33 Stapleton, 'Qualifying Choice', p. 197.
34 Margaret D. Kamitsuka, 2023, *Unborn Bodies: Resurrection and Reproductive Agency*, Minneapolis, MN: Fortress Press, p. 121.
35 Kamitsuka, p. 116.
36 Rapp, *Testing Women, Testing the Fetus*, pp. 89–93.
37 Rapp, *Testing Women, Testing the Fetus*, p. 279.
38 Eilidh Campbell, 2021, *Motherhood and Autism: An Embodied Theology of Motherhood and Disability*, La Vergne: Hymns Ancient & Modern Ltd, p. 109.
39 Campbell, *Motherhood and Autism*, p. 107.
40 Tara Mills, 2024, 'I left my son at school so he'd be taken into care', BBC News online, 24 Sept, https://www.bbc.co.uk/news/articles/c2lnd5wj9z5o, accessed 03.05.2025.
41 Pat Hurst, et al., 2024, '"Devoted" mum and disabled daughter, 8, at centre of Salford murder-suicide probe named', *Manchester Evening News*, 24 Sept, https://www.manchestereveningnews.co.uk/news/greater-manchester-news/mum-daughter-salford-murder-suicide-29996767, accessed 03.05.2025.
42 Rapp, *Testing Women, Testing the Fetus*, p. 159.
43 Rapp, *Testing Women, Testing the Fetus*, p. 307.
44 Abortion: Church of England Statements, https://www.churchof

england.org/sites/default/files/2017-11/abortion-church-of-england-statements.pdf, accessed 02.05.2025.
  45 Rapp, *Testing Women, Testing the Fetus*, p. 131.
  46 Rapp, *Testing Women, Testing the Fetus*, p. 227.

5

# How Do We Talk Pastorally About Abortion?

In the Introduction, it was noted that women can, and do, keep silent about their abortion decisions generally, choosing with care where and how they speak. They are wary of being judged. This may be exacerbated if they are women of faith, concerned that they may be judged both by those they speak to and by God. Abortion stigma, a negative judgement of those who have an abortion, is socially constructed. It may be internalized as well as externally experienced. This means that women who have abortions can feel the need to justify, even if only to themselves, that they are not like the stereotypical idea of a woman who has an abortion. It was noted in the last chapter that women terminating a pregnancy due to a foetal anomaly often wanted to distance themselves from those aborting an unintended pregnancy. They narrate themselves as women who want to be mothers; they just couldn't commit to mothering this child. Kate Cockrill and Adina Nack title their study of abortion stigma 'I'm not that type of person'. They write about women who 'rationalized why the abortion happened and why it was legitimate behaviour despite its taboo'.[1] They describe two methods of rationalization – justification and excuses. 'Excuses allow women to avoid the label of "irresponsibility"; whereas justifications serve women who accept responsibility for their abortions but deny the wrongfulness of the act, therefore denying any negative devaluations of moral character.'[2] Their data suggests a strong correlation between religious affiliation and abortion stigma; they also see a strong connection with idealized views of feminine 'goodness'.

Church statements that either describe all abortion as a serious sin or suggest that it should only happen in exceptional circumstances, inevitably feed into abortion stigma. The exceptionalist position held by the Church of England and The Episcopal Church in the USA both encourage narratives of justification or excuse. To be moral, abortion needs to fit the tragic and rare category, to fit the strictly limited conditions where it is morally preferable to any alternative. Even when the language of sin is not explicitly used, the suggestion that all abortions are tragedies, that they are regrettable and may require repentance, makes it unlikely that women will share their experience if it does not conform to this narrative. If women are discouraged from speaking about their abortions, then their experience will not help challenge the 'tragic' narrative. Abortion secrecy hides the reality of abortion experience and makes changing stereotypes and negative stigma difficult.

## Sin talk

Some Christians might suggest that if women lack remorse, then that is a problem that should be challenged. If the wider society accepts abortion, that does not mean that the Church should. If abortion is understood as a sin, then it follows that women should be encouraged to feel guilt and ask for repentance. The sense of abortion as a sin is explicit in the Roman Catholic Church with rules about how a woman can be received back into the Church through appropriate confession and repentance. Other Churches that hold an exceptionalist view, allowing that some abortions may be moral, give a more ambiguous message. It is not clear if non-exceptional abortions are sinful and how the circumstances are to be judged. The Episcopal Church in the USA holds that abortion should only be used in 'extreme situations'. In the liturgical resources 'Rachel's Tears, Hannah's Hopes', they provide a Rite of Repentance and Reconciliation for an Abortion.[3] This collection of authorized liturgy includes prayers for different experiences of reproductive loss and infertility as well as a selection of prayers around abortion. It was developed in response to a General Convention motion that requested more support for those with post-abortion syndrome. Lauren Winner writes of the prayers for abortion: 'These prayers bespeak shame and remorse. They do not seem to imagine, let alone authorize, other effects or feelings, mixed or unmixed: relief; joy; thanksgiving; nonchalance.'[4] She questions why abortion is the one sin that demands its own rite of penitence. She notes that the prayers either see abortion as a sin that needs confessing so that the woman can be reconciled to God, or as a situation that has left feelings of guilt and shame that God might comfort. She writes, 'if some abortions are sins and some aren't, it isn't the fact that they're abortions that makes them sinful'.

In looking at the history of Christian ideas about sex and abortion, we see that one reason abortion may be considered a sin is because it deliberately interferes with procreation. God is seen as the one who gifts new life, and to prevent or reject that gift is to thwart God's will; thus it is a sin, as it means disobeying God's calling. If the only kind of sex that God approves of is sex that has the potential for conception, then all sexual acts that are deliberately non-procreative fall short of God's ideal. This makes sense of the stance of the Roman Catholic Church and some conservative Protestant Churches against contraception, LGBTQ relationships, and abortion. Yet, many Churches accept the prevention of conception through contraception as responsible family planning. It was noted in Chapter 2 that this responsibility to plan a family is widely understood as a Christian duty of prudence and good stewardship. This is a duty within the marriage relationship where failures in contraception simply mean another child born into a committed relationship. Conception outside of marriage involves sex outside of marriage, which is still seen by most Churches as contrary to God's ideal, especially if the possibility of conception and pregnancy has not been factored in. So, if such sex leads to pregnancy, then the logic may be that the sex was sinful and continuing the pregnancy becomes a form of repentance, even God's way of changing a life. The burden of this is carried by the woman – and perhaps the subsequent child; it has far less impact on the man involved.

If it is God who opens and shuts the womb, then even the unintended conception from 'sinful' sex is God's action to create a new person. Yet, as discussed in Chapter 3, maintaining that each conception is God-ordained raises serious concerns about the fickleness of such gifts. Faithful married couples who long for a child find that they cannot conceive. Pregnancies end in spontaneous miscarriage for reasons that are unclear. Women become pregnant in situations where having a child may be dangerous, distressing or extremely difficult to commit to. If conception is simply due to human biology rather than a direct decision of God, the unfairness of human fertility becomes part of the wider randomness of nature. That an ovum has been fertilized and implanted successfully in the womb means that a new life is beginning. It is possible to recognize God's concern for all life without insisting that God has ordained this particular beginning, to be a particular person, with a preordained future. It is possible to think that sometimes a conception was a mistake, an event that ideally should not have happened. There are different ways of responding to a mistake and one way is to erase it.

Such an erasure means ending what has begun. So, abortion is seen as a sin because it involves killing, or at least stopping the developing life from becoming the baby it would have become. Anti-abortion campaigners talk about 'murder' because this is intentional. They often fail to take into consideration the precarity of early pregnancy and the number of conceptions that end spontaneously. Discussing the status of life in early pregnancy is not clear cut. It is made even more complicated if we consider fertility treatments and the creation of embryos, some of which will never be implanted. Recent attempts to consider even the earliest embryos as equivalent to children in Alabama, USA, has meant that procedures such as IVF are threatened. Discussions of abortion need to happen alongside deepening understanding of spontaneous pregnancy loss and issues of fertility treatments. The complexity of human reproduction means that sometimes conceptions happen, and sometimes they do not, despite a deep desire for children. Some conceptions end spontaneously and sometimes women end them deliberately. All of these women are managing embodied experiences, and all should be met with compassion.

In writing about reproductive injustice, Kathryn Lillian Cox argues for a rethinking of 'sin' talk. 'Specifically, it involves naming as concretely as possible the intersecting network of communal sins influencing individual moral decisions.'[5] She draws on Catholic Social Teaching to explore social and systemic sin in which the majority collude even as they point the finger at individual sinners. The Reformed theologian Serene Jones argues that 'our concepts of sin should never be fashioned or deployed in a manner designed to harm people, to break their spirits, to marginalize them, to destroy their sense of belovedness, or to constrain the conditions of their flourishing'.[6] She sets her understanding of sin firmly within a theology of God's grace. She also stresses that individual actions that may be seen as sinful, falling short, are always held within the wider structures of other people's actions, societal structures and the fallen nature of our world.

> First, sin is both something we do (we sin) and something that happens to us (we are sinned against). Second, sin is something that we consciously enact (sin is wilful) and yet is part of a social reality that we do not will and cannot escape (sin is inescapably social). Third, sin is something experienced by individuals (sin is personal) and yet is corporately enacted and lived (sin is collective).[7]

While it is important to take responsibility for action taken, the choices that we each have are shaped by wider social realities; this includes the behaviour of others and the systemic injustice that can make it hard for individuals to consider different options. An abortion decision is not an abstract one; the individual and societal pressures that shaped the original sexual encounter can affect the decision to abort. Was the woman sinned against by the man? Was she sinned against by the prevailing acceptance of a sexual culture where women are expected to satisfy male pleasure? Societal and religious views of women, of motherhood (including single mothers), of disability, of poverty can all play a part in limiting the choices a woman feels that she can make. In perpetuating impossible norms and devaluing individuals and communities, these systemic cultural pressures can be seen as sinful. Does the inability to imagine dedicating her future life to the care of a severely disabled child reflect the sin of the woman who decides to terminate or the sin of a society that discriminates against disability and fails to provide the support needed to care for a child with complex needs?

Wider political and social attitudes to employment, child-rearing, welfare provision and gender relations can embody structural sins with which we so often, intentionally and unintentionally, collude. As Christians, it is important to recognize where the Church has played a part in creating and maintaining structures of inequality, utilizing stigma and sin talk to judge, control and oppress. The long history of associating sexual pleasure with sin has meant that few Christians have developed coherent and helpful conversation about managing sexual desires. MacCulloch notes how Canon Law from the twelfth to the twentieth centuries banned illegitimate children from ordination as 'part of a general stigmatization of illegitimacy in Western Christianity that has rarely been equalled in intensity in any other culture'.[8] So, the goodness of procreation has been stressed alongside a condemnation of mothers and children who have not conformed to marriage rules. The unrealistic idealization of women's natural maternal nature sets women up to fall short, encouraging levels of self-sacrifice that are rarely expected of men. So, abortion decisions are made within complex structures of sinfulness that reside in human relationships, social systems and community failings, many of which have been shaped by Christian ideas.

Christians must acknowledge our share in human sinfulness

in a fallen world. It can be easy to categorize as sinful a decision that you will never have to make, such as an abortion decision. More complex is acknowledging collusion in the systemic sins that impact such decisions. The aim of this book has been to try and deepen the conversation in ways that recognize the part that historic Christian teachings impact even on current thinking about sex, women and children. These ideas may form embedded theological assumptions about when women's sexual behaviour is considered sinful. Alongside this will be embedded ideas about women's nature and their capacity to care, which may differ from how men are viewed. Is women's sexual desire still considered more problematic than men's? Theological thinking about women's bodies, their sexual desires and what it means to have a reproductive body is still a new field of research. This work recognizes reproductive loss, infertility and the ambiguity many women experience in motherhood. Such work needs to change much inherited sin talk and embedded theological ideas about where sin is located.

Even if the language of sin is not used, the way abortion is spoken about can imply that a good Christian should be able to accept this pregnancy because it is Christian to put the needs of the other first. In the last two chapters, the Annunciation was used in different ways to look at how women might respond to the call of this conception. It was argued that this calling should not be read as a demand from God, so that refusing it would be disobedience. Taking reproductive loss seriously means accepting that each conception is not specifically ordained by God. Mistakes happen and ending a mistaken beginning is not thwarting God's plan. It is not disobeying God's calling. It is a response to a crisis. It may be that aspects of the decision not to welcome a potential life are shaped by self-centred reasons; most decisions are. Yet, suggesting that women should sacrifice their own needs regardless of circumstances is deeply problematic. Women, especially mothers, have been valorized for sacrifices that border on self-abnegation. These can too easily become damaging for both the woman and those she has sacrificed herself for. The self-sacrificial response is not necessarily the best, despite the presumption that women, and particularly mothers, should act sacrificially.

In fact, moving too quickly to self-sacrifice can lead into false binaries of service or selfishness, that can damage women. Brita Gill-Austern writes: 'So women feel forced to choose between self-sacrifice and egoism – between giving up what they have a right to and being primarily concerned with their own interest: between taking seriously others' rights and ignoring the rights of others.'[9] She notes the reflection on the parable of the good Samaritan by Jeanne Stevenson-Moessner, which reminds women that there are limits to what is asked. 'The Samaritan did not give everything away; in this enigmatic parable, he did not injure, hurt or neglect the self.'[10] While feminist pastoral theologians use this parable to note the boundaries of generous care, those writing from a pro-life perspective use it to suggest women should show 'Samaritan'-like love to the life they have conceived and continue a pregnancy whatever the circumstances.

Kamitsuka considers various reflections on the parable and gestational hospitality. She quotes Eugene Schlesinger's eucharistic theology: 'once a believing woman properly understands the meaning of the Eucharist, she will more willingly make the sacrifice and reject abortion'.[11] She considers a number of other theologians, including Stanley Hauerwas, who use the parable equating continuing a pregnancy with Samaritan-like care and concludes,

> The way pro-life authors involve the Samaritan parable trivializes the embodied generosity of even a planned pregnancy, grossly distorts the burdens of carrying an unwanted pregnancy to term and becoming a parent, and overly inflates the kind of practical assistance a church congregation would ever be able to sustain – even if one only looks at the economics.[12]

Sacrifice for the sake of sacrifice is never a constructive choice. Such sacrifices can easily lead to resentment. There needs to be a sense that the sacrifice is both reasonable and worth making.

If a woman's assessment of the situation is that it is not good for this beginning to become a born child in these circumstances, then who is the sacrifice for? The Samaritan's support of the man in need was time limited and merely delayed him on his journey; it did not radically change his life. We are called to give what we can; that may be costly, but it should not destroy us.

Pregnancy means that what is conceived develops from something imperceptible, hidden within the womb, into a being that makes itself felt and 'seen' as it takes up more and more space in the mother's body. All the time it is entirely contingent on her body; it has no possibility of life separate from her. This is a morally unique category not comparable with any other human experience. Todd Peter's argues that this unique category requires a unique term, *prenate*. This term she argues should be adopted and recognized

> as a new moral category to be used instead of person when referring to developing life that occurs inside a woman's body. ... a new way to describe and define the ontological and moral category of the nascent life that exists before a baby takes its first breath.[13]

Perhaps adopting a new term would help in recognizing that this is not like any other situation of dependence, although I am unsure how widely it would be used. At the point of birth, the nascent or potential life becomes a life now separate from the mother, a living, breathing baby. It is no longer held within and fully dependent on her body.

## Exceptionalism

Where the language of sin is not used, such as in the statement of the Church of England, there is still a strong sense of disapproval. In 2017, the last official statement opens by saying: 'The Church of England combines strong opposition to abortion with a recognition that there can be – strictly limited

– conditions under which it may be morally preferable to any available alternative.'[14] This statement offers a pastoral recognition that there will be circumstances where abortion is morally justified. It recognizes that ending a pregnancy is not always wrong. Yet it presumes that in all other situations, it is better for what has been conceived to be born. This means that the reasons for not continuing the pregnancy must be strong enough to counter the view that being born is good. That is why it is assumed that abortion should be strictly limited, although it is not clear who is to do this limiting. Yet, this pro-natal presumption is made by those who have been born; the developing life has no capacity to advocate. I suggest that it is a false premise. It is hard to let go of this presumption when the traditional view is that God is always pro-natal. Nature shows us that not every conception leads to birth. I maintain that it may not always be good for a life that has been conceived to be gestated and born, especially if a woman does not willingly give herself to the process. Why is it presumed that it is good for a child to be born into circumstances where he is unwanted, where she may be resented, where the resources to care for him will be seriously limited or where she may even be in danger?

Of course, if a child is born in such circumstances, there is the possibility that what is needed in terms of love and care will be forthcoming, but we know that this is not always the case. It is important to advocate for provision in society to give all those who have been born the resources necessary for them to thrive. Sometimes, having weighed up the circumstances, a woman decides that it is not good for this life conceived to be gestated and birthed, and so deliberately ends the pregnancy. She decides this long before that life is born, at a stage where she can stop the process. She is not willing or able to give herself to gestating it into a life that could become separate from her. Her reasons will vary, and they may not be considered serious enough by external judges. They may not meet the criteria of those who write church statements.

In thinking pastorally about abortion, the language of

exceptional cases can make it hard for women to talk about their experience. It suggests that they must meet a standard of severity in their situation, a level that is not clearly outlined in any statements made. Those who want to support women through the decision-making will need to accept that sometimes ending a pregnancy is a good decision. If a woman would like to continue the pregnancy but feels that she will not be able to care for a child, conversations about how she might be supported in doing so may be appropriate. If she does not want to continue the pregnancy and does not want this potential child, then helping her to articulate this and to access a safe procedure is appropriate. The reasons why may conform to ideas about exceptional circumstances, but they may not. For her, they reach the threshold; it is better for this pregnancy not to progress and for no child to be born.

## Acknowledging what is lost

This moral decision to end the nascent life in her womb does not mean that a woman considers what is lost to have no value. In Chapters 3 and 4, I noted that women may use different terminology when describing a pregnancy loss that is spontaneous or intentional. For some, this is a baby who has been lost or let go. Others will find different language, or fail to find language, to speak of something that was not yet knowable or of a presence that was deeply unwelcome. In her work as a patient advocate in an abortion clinic, Jeannie Ludlow learned to use the terminology of the woman she was working with. Some referred to getting rid of *it*; few used medical terms such as 'foetus' or 'embryo', though most of the women spoke about 'a baby', a baby that they could not have.[15] The earlier a termination happens, the harder it is to connect what is passed from the body to an actual baby. As most abortions are medically induced, the pregnancy will be lost in the same way as an early miscarriage. The process of heavy bleeding means that what is lost is often passed into the toilet. Sometimes, there will be a recognizable foetus, or foetal sac, among the blood and blood clots that the body expels. Sometimes what is lost will be flushed away without any desire to look. There is no legal, medical or religious requirement to handle what is lost in any particular way.

If the loss happens in a medical setting, then there may be options for the disposal of the pregnancy tissue including cremation or burial. If the abortion is surgical, those performing the termination will handle any pregnancy tissue. It is now rarely disposed of as clinical waste as it used to be. Any foetal remains from a single pregnancy loss will be tiny, so hospitals tend to collect these remains and jointly cremate or bury them in a dignified manner. Individual women may be informed of when this is happening, and they and those supporting them may have the option of attending a service. Pregnancy loss at home, spontaneous or induced, is entirely in the hands of the woman and those with her. She may choose to flush away, dispose of by other means, or bury the remains. She may take what has passed to a medical or funeral setting for them to dispose of it in a dignified way. Formally, before 24 weeks gestation, this loss will not be marked as a baby that has died.

A growing recognition of the grief experienced by many has altered the conversation around pregnancy loss that happens before 24 weeks gestation. As noted in Chapter 3, since 2024, in the UK baby recognition certificates can be requested from the government to mark a pregnancy loss at any stage of gestation. Increasingly, funerals or other religious rituals are offered to those who want to mark their baby's death through miscarriage. It is interesting to note that The British Pregnancy Advisory Service (BPAS), one of the main providers of abortion in the UK, offers advice for those who want to take their foetal remains away after an abortion. As with a spontaneous miscarriage, they can advise about funeral directors or for the personal, private burial of the remains. My presumption is that this is more common in cases of abortion after a prenatal diagnosis, but I do not know if this has been researched. Ludlow writes movingly of the option the clinic she worked at in the USA offered women to view their post-procedure foetus. About

5% of women chose to do this. The experience was carefully managed, ensuring the woman would know what she was seeing and understand the stage of gestation and how little might be observed. She notes that some were curious, some found it helped them with a sense of finality, while others wanted to say goodbye. Occasionally, women would pray or sprinkle the remains with holy water they had brought, simple rituals entrusting this life to their God.[16] In her article she also notes that some clinics offer the means for women to write letters, 'to their fetuses, to other women in the clinic, or to their god telling about their feelings'.[17]

Abortions in the second trimester are less frequent and happen for a number of reasons. The woman may have failed to realize she was pregnant earlier (a particular issue for women taking the pill), she may have needed time to make this decision, or the circumstances of her life have changed in a way that what seemed possible no longer feels possible. Abortions after a prenatal diagnosis of foetal anomalies are often in the second trimester and occasionally even later in pregnancy. This alters the experience of loss, and the physical remains that are lost will look more recognizably baby-like. The stage of development may mean that a baby can be held if so desired, but that depends on the abortion procedure offered. Women terminating after a diagnosis of foetal anomalies are likely to be offered rituals of grief and sometimes mementos of the baby, photographs, footprints. They may well name the baby and speak of their loss to others even if they are circumspect about the actual abortion.

Pastoral responses towards those experiencing pregnancy loss have changed markedly in recent times with a growing awareness of the grief miscarriage can bring. This has changed the way lost pregnancy tissue is treated within clinical settings. As more abortions happen at home, more women are needing to manage the disposal of what is lost, themselves. Within forums that discuss miscarriage, private rituals of handling pregnancy remains and marking the loss of a baby are shared. I am not aware of research that considers whether women devise such rituals after an abortion loss at home. Yet, as with the women Ludlow described, I can easily believe that some treat with reverence what is lost and may even do so with prayers.

## The unborn and the unbaptized

The traditional Christian attitude to the remains of pregnancy loss has been shaped by the theology of ensoulment and baptism. As noted in pervious chapters, an unformed foetus did not have a soul; the foetus was thought to be formed around the fourth month. Any loss in early pregnancy was subject to the same taboos and disgust around menstrual blood. Pregnancy remains were considered filthy.[18] The loss of a formed baby through miscarriage or stillbirth was problematic because this was now an unbaptized soul, and entry to heaven was only for the baptized. Emergency baptism could be performed if it could be claimed that a premature labour had birthed a baby that breathed, even if for a very short time. Otherwise, the stillborn remained unbaptized and could not be buried in consecrated ground. Evidence shows that such babies were often buried privately close to the consecrated ground or in the home, with rituals outwith the Church. Up until the late twentieth century, the Roman Catholic Church still restricted access to burial for the unbaptized. Pastoral concerns have altered the practice. The existence of Limbo, an eternal place for unbaptized babies where they did not suffer but remained outside heaven, has been refuted. Most Catholic dioceses will arrange funerals and burials, no longer suggesting that such lost babies have no place in heaven.

Calvin maintained that baptism was not a requirement of salvation; the unbaptized infants of believing parents were among the elect. His wife had several miscarriages, and they lost an infant son. Kamitsuka notes that the Protestant reformers were both more aware of, and more sympathetic to, pregnancy loss. Yet, she maintains that 'they were unable to conceptualize what the resurrection meant for those beings who died before birth with an undeveloped body'.[19] In her book *Unborn Bodies*, she notes the theological complexity. How does life begun but not formed figure in a theology of bodily resurrection? Can these tiny beginnings have a place in eternity? She is exploring a theology that can comfort a woman who grieves the loss early in pregnancy of her baby with the belief that this life that she never saw or held in her arms will somehow be there in heaven. If it applies to those early pregnancy losses of spontaneous miscarriages, then it applies to abortions. There are complexities to this vision of heaven. Will all those early conceptions unnoticed and ungrieved exist in heaven and what will it mean for those of us who have experienced pregnancy loss, spontaneous or deliberate, who have never considered this a lost baby? What is important is a discussion that begins to consider these issues rather than simply ignoring them. It is possible to hold the belief, as I do, that God does not ordain each conception but still cares for all that is created, however fleeting.

I acknowledge that many who spontaneously miscarry even in the earliest weeks of pregnancy will take comfort from the view that God has taken and cared for their baby. It may also be reassuring to a woman who has decided that she cannot mother this child and so terminates the pregnancy, to believe that the one she cannot love is being loved by God. Popular piety talks about the unborn being with the angels, and the term 'angel baby' is used by some to refer to a baby lost during pregnancy. Kamituska, in developing a theology of emergent resurrection, offers the possibility of the unformed bodies that die in the womb being part of bodily resurrection and thus being knowable in heaven. While it might be comforting for some women, it may be unsettling to others to think that what was lost or what was deliberately aborted will meet them in heaven. Aware of this ambivalence, she writes reassuringly: 'If God does return storied identities to the emergent resurrected bodies of foetuses and their mothers, there will be no recrimination, guilt, or sorrow but acceptance and a peace that "surpasses all understanding".'[20]

## How do we talk about abortion?

Abortion stigma that is fuelled by anti-abortion rhetoric is also shaped by the seemingly more moderate statements of Churches. These are often moralistic in tone, offering a general disapproval of abortion while acknowledging that safe legal access to abortion might sometimes be necessary. It would be helpful for such statements to acknowledge that, within most Church traditions, people will hold different views, not least about what might be considered an exceptional circumstance. While compassion is asked for all involved, there is rarely a link to any kind of theological or liturgical resources. Nor are there any links to organizations who might be able to give support or advice. It would be good to have some form of theological reflection available that might help people thinking through the issues. Some Churches have links to quite dense reports, which tend to have little to say to the person unintentionally pregnant. When abortion is considered principally as an ethical issue, it can lose sight of the pastoral realities. Individuals may search the web to find out what their Church teaches, and mostly they will find position statements. Where there are theological resources, for instance from the Methodist Church and Church of Scotland, they are quite dated. These are matters that need to be up to date in interacting with medical procedures.

As Churches become more aware of the pastoral needs of those who face infertility and spontaneous pregnancy loss, it would be good to see an extension of care to those whose loss is deliberate. Recognizing that the circumstances around such a decision may be complex means that some women may want rituals of loss. It is interesting to note that BPAS offers links to Humanist funeral services after an abortion. How easily would someone find a safe Christian minister? Training is needed in pastorally supporting those engaged in fertility treatment as they make decisions about screening, embryo storage and potential destruction. Conversations about prenatal testing should happen long before couples are faced with decisions even knowing that they will not predetermine those decisions. Such care needs to sit alongside pastoral training around the experience of abortion at different stages of pregnancy. Intelligent informed conversations may well help those who will find themselves making difficult decisions or supporting family members making such decisions.

If the language used in Churches maintains that abortion is only morally acceptable in exceptional situations, then by implication it is possible to differentiate between good and bad abortions, reasonable and trivial reasons. For a woman to tell her abortion story she would need to excuse or justify her decision in line with an exceptional set of circumstances. There would be an inevitable concern about how she was being judged. At some level she would need to self-describe as a victim to find compassion. As noted above, if the predominant Church language is about sin and repentance, then it does not allow a woman to share her experience of relief and gratitude. It is therefore not surprising that women rarely turn to their pastors, priests or ministers to talk about their abortion experiences. This means that those in general pastoral roles do not develop practical wisdom in this area.

Research that counters myths of post-abortion mental health problems is widely accessible, and pastoral training programmes should point people to such research. Those who speak about abortion publicly, especially from the pulpit or other position of Church authority, have a duty to be well informed. The statistics indicate the likelihood of there being women listening for whom this is a life experience or for whom it may be. The language used should not deliberately or inadvertently judge and shame these women. The website and travelling exhibition 'My Body My Life', co-curated by the Open University and Oxford University, enables women to post their abortion stories and offers an insight into the different emotions and experiences of women across the UK.[21] Reading these stories can broaden understanding and challenge stereotypes. Ideally, women of faith should be able to find trustworthy, non-judgemental spiritual support as they make their decision, undergo the process and recover.

## HOW DO WE TALK ABOUT ABORTION?

The rise in medical abortions carried out at home means that the process can be private, but it can also be lonely. Some women will have the support of their partner or of good friends. In many parts of the world, abortion 'doulas', or accompaniers, will be with women physically or virtually to support them through the process. Those with pastoral roles in the Church have often sat with the ill and the dying. There is plenty of wisdom about the liminal space between life and death, and the ability to prayerfully accompany people. Is it possible to envisage offering that same kind of support to a woman having an abortion at home? Being present to assist in offering what has now died to God's mercy, if that is what is wanted? There is much work to be done before women would feel confident in asking for such support, yet I would like to feel that it would be available.

One stereotype of women who have abortions, particularly early abortions, is that they give no moral value to the foetus, seeing it as just some tissue or a clump of cells. While this is how some women process the decision, it is not true of all. Women speak about the baby that they cannot have. Ann Furedi, drawing on years of experience of supporting women through abortions writes that, 'when a woman chooses to end her pregnancy, it is not out of hatred or indifference to the foetus. It is also unlikely to be out of ignorance about what the foetus has the potential to become'.[22] It is possible to accord moral value to the emergent life, even to speak of it as a baby and yet be certain that it is right to end this pregnancy. Until recently, there was little pastoral understanding of any reproductive loss. It was assumed that women who miscarried did not need prayers, rituals or support. Those speaking up from experience are changing that. In doing so, they have sought to show the value of even the earliest pregnancy loss. Prayers and rituals that support them are beginning to be developed.

There may well be women of faith who have abortions who would value liturgies and prayers that are not simply focused on repentance, but could allow them to express complex feelings. Women do pray about their abortion decisions and pray for the life that is lost. This is a life that they could not mother, a beginning that they could not commit to. To acknowledge that does not require guilt for the action taken. Like many decisions, a road has not been taken; in this case, a beginning of life has been ended. There may be guilt, sorrow and regret, but care needs to be taken not to induce these feelings nor to assume where to locate them. A woman may feel neither regret nor repentance, simply relief and gratitude towards those who treated her and supported her. In either case, she may want to trust what has been lost to the mercy and care of God – and to do so in the language she chooses, be that a lost baby or a beginning that ended. She may want to express her sadness at a world that does not make it easy for women, where mothering is both idealized and undervalued.

Human reproduction is not straightforward. The Christian tradition has seen procreation as central to the human vocation, something that God wills and God blesses. Yet in doing so, it has stigmatized those who are unable to have children, those who do not want children and those who have children in the wrong circumstances. This has predominantly affected women and continues to impact women in many Churches today. Not only is motherhood often held up as the primary vocation of women, but such motherhood is meant to be self-sacrificial and natural. Abortion is seen as a negation of God's blessing and of women's nature, a rejection of motherhood. It is also caught up in concerns about sexual behaviour. This means that abortion talk is often sin talk. I have argued that sin talk needs to be used with extreme care and set within the wider understanding of social and systemic sin. It is not possible to separate the abortion decision from the wider societal issues of inequality, including gender violence against women and girls, hyper-sexualization, racism and sexism. Recognizing the ways in which we collude with the unjust systems is where issues of repentance need to be focused. Perhaps if we could begin to have better conversations about all of these issues, we could have better conversations about abortion.

# HOW DO WE TALK ABOUT ABORTION?

## Notes

1 Kate Cockrill and Adina Nack, 2023, 'I'm Not That Type of Person', in Rebecca Todd Peters and Margaret D. Kamitsuka, eds, *Abortion and Religion: Jewish, Christian, and Muslim Perspectives*, London: T&T Clark, p. 67.

2 Cockrill and Nack, 'I'm Not That Type of Person', p. 67.

3 The Episcopal Church, Standing Commission on Liturgy and Music, 2009, *Enriching Our Worship 5: Liturgies and Prayers Related to Childbearing, Childbirth, and Loss*, Supplemental Liturgical Materials, pp. 27–30, https://www.churchpublishing.org/siteassets/pdf/liturgies-and-prayers-related-to-childbearing/enrichingourworship5.pdf, accessed 05.05.2025

4 Lauren F. Winner, 2024, 'A Reading of Abortion in *Enriching Our Worship 5*', *Anglican Theological Review* 106(3), pp. 270–83, https://doi.org/10.1177/00033286241272417, accessed 05.05.2025.

5 Kathryn Lilla Cox, 2024 'Reproductive Injustice as Social Sin: Mapping Sin Discourse into Debates about Fertility Decisions', in Simeiqi He and Emily Reimer-Barry, eds, *Reproduction and the Common Good: Global Perspectives from the Catholic Tradition*, Eugene, OR: Pickwick Publications, p. 94.

6 Serene Jones, 2019, *Trauma + Grace: Theology in a Ruptured World*, 2nd edition, Louisville, KY: Westminster John Knox, p. 102.

7 Jones, *Trauma + Grace*, p. 103.

8 Diarmaid MacCulloch, 2024, *Lower than the Angels: A History of Sex and Christianity*, London: Allen Lane, p. 262.

9 Jeanne Stevenson-Moessner, ed., 1996, *Through the Eyes of Women: Insights for Pastoral Care*, Minneapolis, MN: Fortress Press, p. 311.

10 Stevenson-Moessner, *Through the Eyes of Women*, p. 323.

11 Margaret D. Kamitsuka, 2019, *Abortion and the Christian Tradition: A Pro-Choice Theological Ethic*, Louisville, KY: Westminster John Knox Press, p. 162.

12 Kamitsuka, *Abortion and the Christian Tradition*, p. 168.

13 Rebecca Todd Peters, 2018, *Trust Women: A Progressive Christian Argument for Reproductive Justice*, Boston: Beacon Press, p. 161.

14 Abortion: Church of England Statements, https://www.churchofengland.org/sites/default/files/2017-11/abortion-church-of-england-statements.pdf, accessed 02.05.2025.

15 Jeannie Ludlow, 2008, 'Sometimes It's a Child and a Choice: Toward an Embodied Abortion Praxis', *Feminist Formations*, 20(1), Spring, p. 43.

16 Ludlow, 'Sometimes It's a Child and a Choice', p. 45.

17 Ludlow, 'Sometimes It's a Child and a Choice', p. 44.

18 Margaret D. Kamitsuka, 2023, *Unborn Bodies: Resurrection and Reproductive Agency*, Minneapolis, MN: Fortress Press, p. 35.
19 Kamitsuka, *Unborn Bodies*, p. 49.
20 Kamitsuka, *Unborn Bodies*, p. 131.
21 'My Body My Life', www.mybody-mylife.org, accessed 05.05.2025.
22 Ann Furedi, 2021, *The Moral Case for Abortion: A Defence of Reproductive Choice*, 2nd edn, Basingstoke: Palgrave Macmillan, p. 96.

# Conclusion

Too often, the way that people talk about abortion is in the abstract: whether it is always wrong or in what circumstances it might be acceptable. The aim of this book is to recognize that each abortion decision is made in the context of a unique life situation. Such decisions should not be characterized as women asserting their own rights above those of an innocent child or rejecting motherhood per se, or of rejecting God's gift of this particular new life. Foregrounding women means recognizing the costliness of pregnancy and birth. It also means reflecting on the assumptions that are made about maternal love and the capacity to care. I have argued that abortion decisions draw on women's recognition of the costs of gestating, birthing and bringing up children. The responsibility involved in bringing a new human being to life and then caring for it weighs heavily in these decisions, and sometimes the woman is convinced that this is not a responsibility she can accept. It may be that a level of irresponsibility on her part or the part of another has led to the conception. Maybe not. Deciding not to continue the pregnancy is often a recognition that it would be irresponsible to gestate and birth a child at this time in her circumstances.

It is in the hope of promoting better conversations around the topic of abortion that this book has been written. These conversations are difficult. It is important to listen to those who hold different positions while also challenging myths and prejudices. It would help to move away from the language of sin and repentance that focus on the act of abortion. When the abortion itself becomes the primary topic of sin talk, there is a danger that the systemic sins of society are ignored. The reasons for having an abortion range from an unintended accident in a consensual relationship to more troubled situations that reflect the deep power imbalance that can be present in sexual encounters. The woman may have been sinned against. Societal inequalities play an important part in many abortion decisions. Raising a child is costly, and statistics show that areas of deprivation have higher abortion rates. In the UK, 30% of children were classed as living in relative poverty in 2022/23.[1] Idealized views of motherhood mean that women fear being harshly judged for their failings. Such concerns impact whether a woman believes she can provide what a child needs to flourish.

Research shows that the overwhelming response of a woman to an abortion is relief. She is no longer looking at months of pregnancy. She does not have to negotiate life, work and relationships as an expectant mother. She may be able to continue with her life as planned in terms of education, work and relationships. She may continue to struggle with a life full of difficulties but without the added responsibility of a new baby. The alternative – continuing the pregnancy – is a costly decision. The burden of pregnancy cannot be shared; there is no opportunity for taking a break. There are ways that she can be supported through the months of gestation – practical and emotional help makes a difference – yet she alone carries this developing life in her body, nurtures it and sustains it at some cost to her own health and wellbeing.

It needs to be acknowledged that many of those who have abortions do so because they realize that the responsibility for bringing up a child is immense. Other people can help and share this, although how easily such support is available will be a factor in her decision. Where women lack support, they can find themselves struggling, only to find their shortcomings harshly judged. Society can be quick to condemn mothering that is seen as inadequate. Churches down the ages have played a significant part in stigmatizing women who have children outside of marriage or who fail to conform to an idealized vision of the self-sacrificing mother. Today, society in the UK may be more accepting of single mothers, but that does not mean that women bringing up children alone do not at times still feel unfairly judged. In her essay, Kathryn Lillia Cox tells the story of Miriam, a teenage mother at a Catholic high school. The girl notes that she did not use contraception, which her Church disapproves of, did not have an abortion, and yet having continued the pregnancy and kept her child, she still sometimes finds herself stigmatized as a sinner.[2]

Changing the way that Christians talk about abortion means challenging embedded theology that has shaped attitudes to sexual behaviour and to God's role in reproduction. More theological work is needed to consider how the reality of human sexual desire can be separated from its history of sin and shame. Sexual relationships based on consent that promote mutual respect and aim at mutual pleasure can uphold Christian virtues, enabling responsible self-control. The complex history of marriage, which has often involved the subordination and even ownership of women, needs to be acknowledged rather than simply offered as God's design for humanity. It is good to speak of sexual fidelity and the capacity for physical intimacy to strengthen committed human relationships. Marriages can provide strong and stable partnerships that do good in the world. They are not all about sex. Even in heterosexual relationships, procreative sex will only be a priority for a limited period. As people live much longer lives, there needs to be a theological discussion of how physical intimacy develops across a person's life.

The main theological presumption that I have challenged is the idea that God pre-ordains each conception and that somehow God's purposes are undermined if a conception is deliberately ended. This seems to be at odds with the assumption that God is always pro-birth. In recognizing the precarity of conception and early pregnancy, it becomes hard to suggest that each conception must become a born person. Thinking pastorally about abortion means accepting the randomness of human reproduction and trusting that God is with people

# CONCLUSION

navigating this very human experience in all its complexity. The harsh reality is that many beginnings do not lead to a baby. However people choose to talk about the life in the womb, many conceptions are lost for reasons that are, as yet, unclear. The grief of pregnancy loss should not be used to negate women in very different situations choosing to induce such a loss. Abortion should not be considered as a separate topic in opposition to wider discussions of birth and motherhood. It is timely that theologians are beginning to reflect on the complex world of human reproduction from women's perspectives, not least because issues around fertility treatments, embryo research, miscarriage and prenatal screening are also becoming increasingly complex.

When I began to explore the theology of motherhood in the early 2000s, I was shocked to find so little to read. Despite millennia of Christian theology maintaining that motherhood was the prime vocation for women, the assumption was that it simply happens. God, it is suggested, designed women to be mothers, and therefore women do so naturally. Listening to women suggests that it is more complicated. There is more published work now, but it is still considered a niche field. Currently, women are writing and researching the topics of infertility, pregnancy loss, childbirth – including birth trauma, post-natal depression and the joys, ambivalence and sheer hard work of bringing up children. It is the contention of this book that abortion belongs in this mix. Women who struggle to have the children they want, who grieve the loss of miscarriage, who navigate the physical, emotional and ethical issues of IVF and who listen to the Bible stories of miraculous births, need better pastoral support and a deeper understanding of their experience. So do women who find themselves unintentionally pregnant, who need to take stock of their situation and question whether they can bring a child to birth at this time.

Many who have a view on abortion will never face an abortion decision themselves. Yet, they may be in a position to listen to someone processing their experience or to offer pastoral support prior to, during or after an abortion. This means that they need to be compassionate to the woman's situation, slow to judge and open to understand. Women facing an unintended pregnancy or changing circumstances within a planned pregnancy should be able to draw on non-judgemental pastoral support, and it would be good if such support was relatively easy to find. They may need to rethink their future, to make the space necessary and commit to this new life. They may be struggling with a diagnosis that makes this child different from the one they had expected. They need to know more about the particular condition, more about the child's different needs and how they can or cannot envision this future. The support these women want might be spiritual, emotional and practical. It may include talking about ending the pregnancy. If so, their reasons need to be taken seriously, their concerns listened to and their final decision respected. This may involve being with them for appointments or when they lose the pregnancy. It may involve offering prayers, rituals and a dignified resting place for what is lost. How such endings are received by God is a mystery, though we can always trust in God's merciful love. Decisions about whether to continue or end a pregnancy are time sensitive, so those who might be called on to offer pastoral support need to have thought about these issues in advance or at least know where to get information.

As with so many human situations in our fallen world, random nature, human actions, sin, personal and systemic, can all play a part in the beginnings and endings of pregnancy. A pastoral response involves helping to locate the grace, mercy and compassion of God for all of those involved. An abortion is not a general rejection of motherhood. It might be that this is not the right time for the woman to be a mother; it is too early, or too late. The complexity of her life may mean that she cannot envisage bringing a child into it. She may be clear that she does not want this man's baby. She may lack the resources, material, emotional or practical, to be the kind of mother she thinks this child needs. Some women who have abortions already have children they are caring for. Some women who have abortions will go on to have children at a different point in their life, perhaps with a different person. Their capacity to mother those children will not be any the less because they have decided not to continue this pregnancy. Issues beyond the immediate decision may be more pressing and require more support.

The theological work being done around the complexity of human reproduction is mainly being done by women theologians. Yet, both men and women make statements about the rights and wrongs of abortion, so it is vital that men engage with these topics too. This applies especially to ideas of God's providence and questions of systemic sin. To locate sin specifically in the act of abortion is a failure to recognize the sinful systems of inequality that many of us collude in. Men are involved in the sex that leads to conception and in societal views about sex and sexual behaviour. Educating men and boys in sexual behaviour that respects women and their pleasure is one way to begin to challenge the power dynamics in many sexual encounters. Men are often involved in caring for children. They may experience the grief of infertility and of reproductive loss. They may impact abortion decisions, either by being supportive or by their lack of commitment. Continuing to challenge stereotypes that assume women are more able to care for children than men is also necessary for a greater sharing of the burdens of parenting in whatever situation. Theologies of sex and gender that overemphasize women's maternal role need to be problematized, not to negate the value of mothering but to recognize that all humans have the capacity to care. Such caring needs to be learned and practised, and is not always easy. Financial pressures, working expectations and waiting for the right time and person to commit, all factor into the lives of young adults and the decisions they make about becoming parents. Statistics show that it is in this age group that the majority of unintended pregnancies end in abortions.

In her book *Trust Women*, Todd Peters[3] reminds readers that pregnancy is a unique moral category. There is no other life experience in which a developing life is entirely contingent on the life of its mother. It is because of this unique situation that she and I maintain that abortion decisions should principally be the decision of that woman. Only she can gestate this new life and birth it into the world. Sometimes, when I have conversations about abortion, I am told that all will be simpler when there are artificial wombs – then a woman will not have to continue a physical pregnancy; she can simply hand it over. No longer will gestation require the bodily generosity of an individual woman. I know that already life can begin outside the womb and pre-term babies can survive with skilful medical care and sophisticated equipment. I am assured that in time the whole complex bodily process of gestating a life will be perfected, although I have my doubts of how the physicality of pregnancy will be replicated. Yet, if and when that happens, new inequalities will begin. It will be costly; difficult questions will be raised about screening embryos and who gets access to the most sophisticated, state-of-the-art wombs. Who knows what the problems might be for the ones who get a cheaper option. An old-fashioned womb in a woman's body will always be much cheaper. It may well change what it means to be human and change many things about what it is to be male and female.

For now, pregnancy happens in women's bodies. A woman who conceives needs to give herself bodily to the making of a new human being and will find herself becoming a mother. Sometimes a woman decides that she cannot continue her pregnancy and will look for a safe way to end it. If there is not a safe way, she may well feel driven to try unsafe procedures – and that may cost her her life. The premise of this book is that abortions have always happened, and they continue to be a part of human reproductive experience. Nowadays, it is possible to end a pregnancy in a way that is safe for the woman. Legislation may aim to prevent abortion, limit access or limit the grounds, but it does not stop women ending their pregnancies. It may mean that they struggle to find safe access; it may mean abortions happen later in pregnancy, that women travel to access them or that they resort to unsafe procedures.

# CONCLUSION

Telling women that abortion is sinful – even that they have excommunicated themselves by having one – does not stop women from having abortions. Increasing pre-abortion counselling, showing women scan pictures or making them listen to a foetal heartbeat does not stop women having abortions. Protesting outside clinics, calling women 'murderers' and harassing the staff who carry out procedures has not reduced the abortion rates. No woman aspires to having an abortion; it is not on anyone's wish list. Women find themselves in situations where abortion enables them to end a pregnancy that they want ended. The reasons why will be multifaceted. Tackling these reasons will mean addressing intersecting inequalities. It will also mean accepting that human reproduction is fickle, and however we perceive God's role in the process, the unfairness of infertility, pregnancy loss and unintended conception all need to be factored in. Finding ways of offering pastoral care in these situations needs nuanced engagement, up-to-date knowledge and compassionate understanding.

## Notes

1 End Child Poverty, 'Child Poverty Statistics 2024', https://endchildpoverty.org.uk/child-poverty-2024/, accessed 24.04.2025.

2 Kathryn Lilla Cox, 2020, 'Reproductive Injustice as Social Sin: Mapping Sin Discourse into Debates about Fertility Decisions', *Journal of Moral Theology* 6 (CTEWC Book Series 6), pp. 90–121, https://doi.org/10.55476/001c.124019, accessed 24.04.2025.

3 Rebecca Todd Peters, 2018, *Trust Women: A Progressive Christian Argument for Reproductive Justice*, Boston: Beacon Press.

# Select Bibliography

Beattie, Tina, 2009, 'Catholicism, Choice and Consciousness: A Feminist Theological Perspective on Abortion', *International Journal of Public Theology* 4(1), pp. 51–75, https://doi.org/10.1163/187251710X12578338897863, accessed 01.05.2025.

Brock, Brian, 2020, *Wondrously Wounded: Theology, Disability, and the Body of Christ*, SRTD: Studies in Religion, Theology, and Disability, Waco, TX: Baylor University Press.

Brooke, Stephen, 2001, '"A New World for Women"? Abortion Law Reform in Britain during the 1930s', *The American Historical Review* 106(2), April, pp. 431–59, https://doi.org/10.2307/2651613, accessed 01.05.2025.

Brown, Peter Robert Lamont, 1988, *The Body and Society: Men, Women and Sexual Renunciation in Early Christianity*, Lectures on the History of Religions, 13, New York: Columbia University Press.

Cahill, Ann J., 2015, 'Miscarriage and Intercorporeality', *Journal of Social Philosophy* 46(1), March, pp. 44–58, https://doi.org/10.1111/josp.12082, accessed 01.05.2025.

Chambers, K. Lindsey, 2020, 'It's Complicated: What Our Attitudes toward Pregnancy, Abortion, and Miscarriage Tell Us about the Moral Status of Early Fetuses', *Canadian Journal of Philosophy* 50(8), November, pp. 950–65, https://doi.org/10.1017/can.2020.48, accessed 01.05.2025.

Furedi, Ann, 2021, *The Moral Case for Abortion: A Defence of Reproductive Choice*, 2nd edn, Basingstoke: Palgrave Macmillan.

Gill, Robin, 2021, 'Church of England (Anglican) Perspectives on Abortion', in Alireza Bagheri, ed., *Abortion: Global Positions and Practices, Religious and Legal Perspectives*, Cham: Springer International Publishing, pp. 63–72, https://doi.org/10.1007/978-3-030-63023-2_6, accessed 23.05.2025.

Jones, Serene, 2019, *Trauma + Grace: Theology in a Ruptured World*, 2nd edn, Louisville, KY: Westminster John Knox, p. 102.

Hansen, Danielle Tumminio, ed., 2024, 'Anglican Theologies of Reproductive Choice', *Anglican Theological Review* 106(3), pp. 233–6, https://journals.sagepub.com/toc/atra/106/3, accessed 01.05.2025.

Hopwood, Nick, Rebecca Fleming and Lauren Kassell, eds, 2018, *Reproduction: Antiquity to the Present Day*, Cambridge: Cambridge University Press.

Kamitsuka, Margaret D., 2019, *Abortion and the Christian Tradition: A Pro-Choice Theological Ethic*, Lousiville, KY: Westminster John Knox Press.

———, 2023,*Unborn Bodies: Resurrection and Reproductive Agency*, Minneapolis, MN: Fortress Press.

Kandiah, Michael, and Gillian Staerck, 2002, *The Abortion Act 1967*, London: Institute of Contemporary British History.

King, Helen, ed., 1998, *Hippocrates' Woman: Reading the Female Body in Ancient Greece*, London: Routledge.

———, 2024, *Immaculate Forms: Uncovering the History of Women's Bodies*, London: Profile Books.

Lindemann, Hilde, 2016, *Holding and Letting Go: The Social Practice of Personal Identities*, Oxford/New York/Auckland: Oxford University Press.

Ludlow, Jeannie, 2008, 'Sometimes, It's a Child and a Choice: Toward an Embodied Abortion Praxis', *Feminist Formations* 20(1), Spring, pp. 26–50.

MacCulloch, Diarmaid, 2024, *Lower than the Angels: A History of Sex and Christianity*, London: Allen Lane.

Mackenzie, Catriona, 1992, 'Abortion and Embodiment', *Australasian Journal of Philosophy* 70(2), June, pp. 136–55, https://doi.org/10.1080/00048409212345041, accessed 01.05.2025.

Mehta, Samira, 2018, 'Family Planning Is a Christian Duty: Religion, Population Control, and the Pill in the 1960s', in Gillian Frank, Bethany Moreton and Heather R. White, eds, *Devotions and Desires: Histories of Sexuality and Religion in the Twentieth-Century United States*.

O'Donnell, Karen, 2022, *Dark Womb: Re-Conceiving Theology through Reproductive Loss*, London, UK: SCM Press.

Page, Sarah-Jane, and Pam Lowe, 2024, *Abortion and Catholicism in Britain: Attitudes, Lived Religion and Complexity*, Palgrave Studies in Lived Religion and Societal Challenges, Cham, Switzerland: Palgrave Macmillan.

Parsons, Kate, 2010, 'Feminist Reflections on Miscarriage, in Light of Abortion', *IJFAB: International Journal of Feminist Approaches to Bioethics* 3(1), March, pp. 1–22, https://doi.org/10.3138/ijfab.3.1.1, accessed 01.05.2025.

Peters, Rebecca Todd, 2018, *Trust Women: A Progressive Christian Argument for Reproductive Justice*, Boston: Beacon Press.

Peters, Rebecca Todd, and Margaret D. Kamitsuka, eds, 2023, *Abortion and Religion: Jewish, Christian, and Muslim Perspectives*, London: T&T Clark.

Rapp, Rayna, 1999, *Testing Women, Testing the Fetus: The Social Impact of Amniocentesis in America*, New York: Routledge.

Reader, Soran, 2008, 'Abortion, Killing, and Maternal Moral Authority', *Hypatia* 23(1), March, pp. 132–49, https://doi.org/10.1111/j.1527-2001.2008.tb01169.x, accessed 01.05.2025.

Reagan, Leslie J., 2010, *Dangerous Pregnancies: Mothers, Disabilities, and Abortion in Modern America*, Berkeley: University of California Press.

———, 1997, *When Abortion Was a Crime: Women, Medicine, and Law in the United States, 1867–1973*, Berkeley: University of California Press.

Thatcher, Adrian, ed., 2014, *The Oxford Handbook of Theology, Sexuality, and Gender*, Oxford: Oxford University Press.

# Index of Bible References

Old Testament

*Genesis*
2                6
3.16             6

*Exodus*
21.22–25        30

New Testament

*Matthew*
13.1–23         11
19.12            8

*1 Corinthians*
7.5              8

*1 Timothy*
2.15             6

# Index of Names and Subjects

abortion
  acknowledging loss 123–6
  alternatives to 72–3
  attitudes towards x
  capacity to mother 104
  Catholic opposition to 29
  complexity of issues
    ix–xxiv
  conservative churches
    against 115–17
  contraception failure 51
  the decision xiii–xv, 57,
    64–6, 139
  difficult conversations
    about 134–41
  exceptionalism 105–6, 114,
    121–3, 129
  historical perspective 26–7
  individual situations
    xiv–xv, 47–8, 74–7, 138–9
  inequality of access 50
  as killing 59–60
  loneliness of 130–1
  as maternal decision 29, 48,
    68–71
  as medical decision 79–89,
    107–9
  moral authority 73
  myths of xii
  as negation of God's will
    131
  non-viable pregnancies 81
  not an abstract decision
    117–18
  not rejecting motherhood
    138
  pastoral needs 128
  premarital sex and 1
  regret and 74–5
  as a relief 135
  responsible parenting xviii
  returning to Churches
    114–15
  to save mother 26
  secret 34–5
  sex selection 94
  sin and 21–3
  stigma of 113–14, 118, 128
  as taboo topic x–xi
  thalidomide and rubella 83,
    84–9
  uncomfortable binaries
    105–6
  for vanity 32
  woman's decision 71–2
  *see also* abortion laws;

abortion methods;
abortion statistical data;
anti-abortion movements;
disabilities; miscarriage;
pregnancy; sex; sin;
women
*Abortion: an Ethical Discussion* (C of E Board of Social Responsibility) 43
*Abortion in the Christian Tradition* (Kamitsuka) xvi
Abortion Law Reform Association (ALRA) 39–41
  horror at unsafe abortions 50
  thalidomide abortions 85
abortion laws
  Abortion Act, UK 26
  anti-poison laws 33–4
  Comstock Law 34
  criminalizing abortion 15
  disability and 88
  exceptional/'therapeutic' 84–9
  gradualist view and 62
  language and disability 92
  legalization xix, 39–41, 39–44
  limits on abortion ix
  made illegal 33–5
  moral discussion xvi
  Offences Against the Person 27–8
  opposing views and xxiii
  removal of quickening 49
  rights and xix, 29, 46, 51
  Roe vs Wade 29, 89
abortion methods 26, 39
  Comstock Law 34
  dangers of 35
  development of drugs 45
  early remedies 31–2
  medication 61
  mifepristone 45
  misoprostol 45
  surgical 61, 93
  unsafe practices xvi, 5, 41–2, 49, 50
abortion statistical data
  before 10 weeks xxi
  attitude survey x
  contraception failure 51
  deprivation and 56, 135
  Down's syndrome 82
  incidence of xii
  marriage and 56
  maternal deaths 45
  previous children 71
  race and ethnicity 76
  teenage pregnancy and 56
  women on their decisions xiv–xv
Abraham, male lineage and 4
Act of Paul (apocryphal book), Thecla and 9
Acts of the Apostles 9
Adam
  marriage and 14
  sex/no sex in Paradise 10, 12
adoption
  abandonment feelings 73

# INDEX OF NAMES AND SUBJECTS

alternative to abortion 72–3
homes 36
adultery
  Christianity and 7
  contraception and 36
  as a crime 15
  disrupting lineage 4
  shifting views on 17–18
African American women 46
alcohol and health in
  pregnancy 80
Ambrose, Bishop of Milan
  clerical celibacy 11
  influence on Augustine 12
American Medical
  Association 33
American Society of Human
  Genetics (ASHG) 94
Andolsen, Barbara H. 19
Anglican Church/Church of
  England
  accepting abortion 28
  Book of Common Prayer 15
  cautious support 44, 50
  contraception and 27
  disability and 88
  evolving views of
    marriage 15–19
  exceptionalism 105, 114,
    121–3
  General Synod 2024
    on disability 82, 98
  *Issues in Human Sexuality*
    20
  Lambeth Conference, 1908
    against contraception
    37–8, 39

Lambeth Conference, 1958
  endorsement of
    contraception 49
  responsible parenting
    42–3
  ordination of women 16
  Prayer Book 16
  'rather you didn't' position
    47–8
  reasons for marriage 17
  responsible parenting xviii
  *Something to Celebrate:*
  *Valuing Families* 17
anti-abortion movements
  organizations and xiii
  pro-life/pro-choice binary
    xix
  religious belief and x–xi
  rhetoric of 128
  talk of 'murder' 116
  *see also* abortion laws
Aristotle 30
Augustine of Hippo
  on sex and sin 12–13, 13–14
  sex without lust 10
  unbaptized infants 31
  wonder at creation 98–9
  autism 102–3

Baird, Professor Dugald 42
Beattie, Tina
  birth of mother and child
    58
  period of grace 61–3
  birth trauma 137
  bodily autonomy of women
    ix

Book of Common Prayer, on marriage 15
Britain *see* United Kingdom
British Pregnancy Advisory Service (BPAS)
  foetal remains and 124–5
  links of Humanist services 128
Brock, Adam 98–9
Brock, Brian
  attitude of wonder 93
  the calling 103
  on wonder and disability 98–9, 100, 101
Brookes, Stephen 39–41
Brown, Peter 9–10
Browne, Stella 40

Cahill, Ann 58–9
Calvin, John
  sex as procreation 14
  the unbaptized foetus 126
Campbell, Eilidh
  *Motherhood and Autism* 102–3
Canada, legal abortion in 45
Catholic Social Teaching 117
Chambers, K. Lindsay
  'It's Complicated' 65
  on regret 74–5
Chance, Janet 40–1
chastity
  clerical 11
  on consecrated virginity 9–10
  early Christianity and 8–14

LGBTQ relationships 20
Mary's virginity and 11
saints and martyrs 13
as superior way 14
*Chicago Times*
  secret abortion investigation 34–5
child abuse 15
children
  abandonment of 33
  child-rearing work 137
  illegitimacy stigma 2, 5, 55, 118, 135
  women's careers and 20
  *see also* conception and procreation; foetuses; infant mortality; parenting
chorionic villus sampling (CVS) 91
Christianity
  chastity and 2, 8–14, 11, 35
  children as God's gift xvii
  on desire 2–23
  God's will and procreation 131
  Jewish roots 6
  marriage 4–7
  persecutions and martyrs 9
  procreation as purpose 27
  Protestantism and sex 14–16
  punishment for harming pregnancy 30–1
  sex and marriage 14–19
  sin 21–3, 114–21
  soul and body 30
  stigma and 118, 135–6

# INDEX OF NAMES AND SUBJECTS

support for choices  109
theology of motherhood
  137
unbaptized foetuses  31,
  126–7
value of prayers for women
  130
views of women  4–7, 19–23
women and theology  16,
  139
*see also* Anglican Church/
  Church of England;
  Church of Scotland;
  Protestant churches;
  Roman Catholic Church
Church of England *see*
  Anglican Church/Church
  of England
Church of England Board of
  Social Responsibility
  *Abortion: an Ethical
  Discussion*  43
Church of Scotland, abortion
  and  28, 128
Cockrill, Kate  113
compassion for women's
  situations  137–8
Comstock Law  34
conception and procreation
  circumstances of  69
  falling birth rate  47
  God's provision  70, 75
  interference with  115–17
  Protestantism and sex
    14–16
  purpose of sex  17, 18
  without lust  10–11

concubinage  15
contraception  21
  abstinence as  35–6
  access to  xix, 56, 76
  churches against  115
  Comstock Law  34
  condoms and  38
  failure of  xxi, 51, 56
  hormonal  46–7
  methods  46–7
  outside marriage  38–9
  preventing, not taking, life
    48
  prostitution and  49
  shifting views of  18, 23, 27,
    35–9, 55
  side effects of  56
  surgical sterilization  47
  types of  50
  wrong motives for  38
  *see also* conception and
    procreation; Roman
    Catholic Church
Cottrell, Stephen, Archbishop
  of York  82
Cox, Kathryn Lillian  117,
  136

dancing: on Witte's crime
  list  15
*The Dark Womb* (O'Donnell)
  xvii, 64
  God's plan and loss  60–1
depression, post-natal  137
disabilities
  abortion as medical decision
    79–89

accidents or illness 99, 104
affirming dignity of disabled 82
capacity to mother 104
caring and 80
caring for children 101–4
changing attitudes towards 107
chromosomal anomalies 81, 107
cultural judgements 93
devaluing children 106
discriminating decisions 94–8
ethics of prevention 107–9
eugenics 79–80, 96
exceptionalism 105–6
God's wonders and 98–9
legal language and 92
medical advancements and 87
perceived 'normality' 95
prenatal screening 107–8
reasons for 80–1
rubella and 83, 85–9, 106–7
screening and testing xxi, 81, 89–93, 94
siblings 102
spina bifida 80, 91, 97
stigma xxi
support for 109
support organizations 92–3
thalidomide and 83, 84–9
women blamed for 5
see also Down's syndrome
'Don't Screen Us Out' campaign 96

Down's syndrome
  abortion statistics 82
  'Don't Screen Us Out' 95–6
  invasive testing 92
  non-invasive testing 94
  prenatal screening 91
Duke, James O.
  *How to Think Theologically* (with Stone) xvi

education
  health and disability 87
  of women 16
Elizabeth, fertility of 4
El Salvador 46
embryos
  as equivalent to children 116
  IVF and 44, 50, 116, 128, 137
  personhood questions xx
  research 44
  see also foetuses
Episcopal Church
  exceptionalism 114
  repentance and reconciliation 114
eugenics 107
eunuchs, Jesus comments on 8
European Society of Human Genetics (ESHG) 94
Eve
  marriage and 14
  punishment of 6
  sex/no sex in Paradise 10, 12

# INDEX OF NAMES AND SUBJECTS

exceptionalism 129
  Churches and 114
  concepts of 121–3

families
  changing 'traditional' 45–6
  planning 35, 41
  preserving honour 32
  see also children; parenting
feminism
  ALRA campaign 40
  perspective on abortion xv, xix, 50
  sacrifice and obligation 101–2
Fergusson, David 70
fertility
  embryos and 128
  fickle and random 60
  historical perspective 27
  IVF treatment xvii, 44, 50, 137
  judgement and 5
  medical advancements 16
  random and unpredictable 116
  theology and xvii
  treatments 116–17
  unfair lottery 64–5
  unpredictable 4
Finkbine, Sherri, thalidomide abortion and 85, 97
foetuses
  anomalies in xi, 79–80, 125
  co-creation with mother 58
  gradualist notion 43–4, 50, 62

  loss and xix–xxi
  moral value of 130–1
  personhood 31, 62–3, 65–9
  quickening 31, 48
  remains of 123–6
  rituals to mark loss xi
  social understanding of personhood 66–8
  soul and 30
  unbaptized 126–7
  'unformed'/'formed' 31
folic acid, spina bifida and 80, 97
foundling and unwed mothers homes 33, 36
'Magdalene houses' 14
Francis, Pope 19
Furedi, Ann
  on contraception 56
  potential child 71

Gabriel, Angel 58–9
Galen 30
gender violence 131
Genesis, Adam and Eve and 14–16
German measles/rubella 83, 85–9, 106–7
Gill, Robin 43–4
Gill-Austern, Brita 120
God
  always pro-natal 122
  merciful love 138
  procreation as central to 131
  provides conception 70, 75, 136
  rejecting gift of 115–17

the unbaptized foetus and 127
Greco-Roman world
  knowledge of pregnancy 30
  male-female bodies and 6–7
Gregory IX, Pope 14
guilt feelings xiv–xv

Habgood, John (later Archbishop) 43–4
Halappanavar, Savita 92
Hannah, fertility of 4
Hauerwas, Stanley 19, 120
Hosea, Book of: wife plays harlot 7
*How to Think Theologically* (Stone and Duke) xvi
Hudson-Wilkin, Rose, Bishop of Dover 17
Humanists 128

immigration 46
incest as a crime 15
inequality 131
  abortion incidence and 76
  systemic issues of xxii
infant mortality 48
  falling in 1930s 40
  historical perspective 27
infanticide 15, 33
  unmarried mothers and 36
Ireland, Republic of, Halappanvar case and 92
*Issues in Human Sexuality* (Church of England) 20
'It's Complicated' (Chambers) 65

Jelen, Ted G. 1
Jenkins, Alice 40
Jesus Christ
  born of a virgin 12
  on eunuchs 8
John Paul II, Pope
  *Mulieres Dignitatum* 19
Jones, Serene 117
Judaism
  disabilities and abortion 88–9
  disability and abortion 86
  fertility from God 6

Kamitsuka, Margaret D.
  *Abortion in the Christian Tradition* xvi
  agency of mother 58
  the good Samaritan 120
  historical Christian thinking 62
  mothering decision 68, 109
  shame and sex 13
  on theology and disability 100–1
  the unbaptized foetus 126–7
  *The Unborn Bodies* 127
  woman's moral authority 73
King, Helen
  abortion remedies 32
  Greek and Roman medicine 30

LGBTQ
  trans men and pregnancy xxii, 2

# INDEX OF NAMES AND SUBJECTS

LGBTQ relationships
  Bishop of Dover on 17
  Christianity's antipathy to 23
  church recognition of 20
  against conception 115
  decisions about parenthood 2
  sexual continence and 20
*Life* magazine, on disabled children 86
Lindemann, Hilda 66–8, 71
Living Out charity 20
loss
  acknowledging 123–6
  deliberate choice and 64–6
  different situations 137
  disability and 106
  foetal anomalies 96
  foetal remains 123–6
  God's plan and 60–1
  grief and 63–4
  holding the baby 93
  individual circumstances 75
  rituals to mark xi
  stillbirth 64
  support after 45
  the unbaptized 126–7
  women's experience of xx
Lowe, Pam
  abortion as taboo topic x–xi
  Catholic pastoral care xiii
Ludlow, Jeannie 126
  language and loss 123
  'Sometimes It's a Child and a Choice' xx

Luther, Katharine 14
Luther, Martin 14

McCabe, Meagan K. 18
MacCulloch, Diarmaid
  martyrdom and virginity 11
  on *'porneia'* 7
  prostitution 14
  punishment for sex crimes 15–16
  shame and sex 13
  on stigma of illegitimacy 118
McKenzie, Catriona 57–60
Malthus, Thomas 37
Marjorie of Kemp 13
marriage and relationships
  Book of Common Prayer 15
  Christian 4–7
  discussion and 21
  later years 35–6
  multiple pregnancies 41
  polygamy as a crime 15
  procreation 10–11
  purpose of 23
  sex within 38
  widowhood and celibacy 10
  *see also* families; parenting
Mary, mother of Jesus
  agency of 58–9
  call of conception 119
  'fear not' 99
  virginity of 2, 11, 13
Mary Magdalene and 'Magdalene houses' 14

Mehta, Samira 42–3
men
  in abortion decisions 139
  celibacy 8–13, 9–10
  inequalities in relationships
    1–2
  learning control 19–20
  lineage of 4
  pornography and 18
  power relations with
    women xxii
  sex education for 139
  sexual moderation 7
  trust/control of women 3–7
mental health
  guilt feelings and xiv–xv
  myth of abortion and
    xii–xv
Methodist Church
  accepting abortion 28
  position statement 128
#MeToo movement 18
miscarriage
  baby loss certificate 64
  development problems 80
  experience of 63–4
  loss and 106
  spontaneous 4
  thalidomide and 84
  theology and xvii
  unclear reasons for 116
  unpredictable 48
mistresses, unacknowledged
  children of 5
Moltmann-Wnedal, Elisabeth
  68
Morgan, Heather Renée 98

mortality, maternal 57
motherhood *see* parenting;
  women
*Motherhood and Autism*
  (Campbell) 102–3
*Mulieres Dignitatum* (John
  Paul II) 19
'My Body My Life'
  exhibition 129

Nack, Adina 113
National Centre for Social
  Research x
Nicaragua 46

O'Donnell, Karen
  *The Dark Womb* xvii,
    60–1, 64
Open University
  'My Body My Life'
    exhibition (with Oxford U)
    129
Oppenheimer, Helen 59
Origen of Alexandria 8
Oxford University
  'My Body My Life'
    exhibition (with OU) 129

Page, Sarah-Jane
  abortion as taboo topic
    x–xi
  Catholic pastoral care xiii
Paintin, Dr David
  close view of abortions
    41–2
  legal abortion saves lives
    44–5

# INDEX OF NAMES AND SUBJECTS

parenting
  abortion not a rejection of 138
  inequalities 1
  knowledge of paternity 2
  maternal decisions xviii
  responsible 42–3, 51
  support for disabled child 101
  theology of motherhood 137
Park, Katharine 32
Parsons, Kate 65–6
pastoral care
  absence in Georgia xii
  Catholic priests and xiii
  circumstances of abortions xiv–xv
  deliberative theology xvi–xvii
  misinformation and xxii
  religion and xxii
  reluctance to turn to xi
  theology of sex 2–23
  women's circumstances 138–41
Patau syndrome 91
Paul, Doris 109
Paul, on marriage 8
Paul VI, Pope
  *Humane Vitae* 44
Peeler, Amy 59
Peters, Rebecca Todd 121
  *Trust Women* 139–40
  well-being of potential child 69–72
Pius IX, Pope 49

Pius XI, Pope
  *Casti Conubii* 39
Poland 46
population growth 37
poverty and deprivation
  abortion incidence and 76
  disabilities and caring 103
  maternal death rates and 57
pregnancy
  acceptance of 57
  artifical womb speculation 140
  co-creation of foetus 58
  conception 3–4
  consent to 3, 54–5
  consequences for women 22, 57–60
  early endings 60–6
  fear of 39
  health advice 80, 97
  marking loss xi
  maternal mortality 48
  maternity care 76
  multiple 41
  older mothers 80, 96, 102
  Old Testament fines 30–1
  period of grace 61–3
  the 'prenate' 121
  reasons to delay 46–7
  spontaneous loss xv
  support instead of abortion 72–3
  ultrasound scans 81
  varied experiences of xx
  woman's vital role xv
prostitution
  abortion and 32–3

'against God' 7
contraception and 32–3, 49
as a crime 15
as non-procreative 14
unsanctioned 5
Protestant churches
  abortion for disabilities
    88–9
  accept contraception 42–3
  conservative anti-abortion
    46
  contraception and 27
  disability and abortion 86
  on procreation 115
Puerperal Fever 41

race and ethnicity 131
  higher numbers of abortion
    76
  maternal death rates and 57
  Reproductive Justice
    movement 46
Rachel, fertility of 4
rape/unconsented sex xxiii
  children of 5
  'rape culture' 18
Rapp, Rayna
  capacity to mother 104
  cultural judgements 93
  disability and 90, 101, 108
Reader, Soran
  abortion as killing 59–60
  maternal decision 68–9
  violation of unwanted
    pregnancy 73
  woman's decision 72
Reagan, Leslie

abortion for disabilities 86,
  88–9
feminism and abortion 41
health education 87
laws xix, 28–9, 33
on Sanger's birth control 36
religion
  God's decisions about
    fertility xvii
  influence on abortion
    attitudes x
  integrating in pastoral care
    xxii
  marking loss of pregnancy xi
  moral discussion xvi
  *see also* Christianity; God;
    Judaism
Reproductive Justice
  movement 29, 46, 76
Riddle, John 32
Roe vs Wade 29, 89
Roman Catholic Church
  against abortion x–xi, 29,
    46, 55
  against contraception 27,
    29, 39, 49, 50, 55, 115
  disability and foetal
    anomalies 86, 88
  modern society and 18
  Paul VI, *Humane Vitae* 44
  Pius IX on soul at
    conception 49
  Pius XI, *Casti Conubii* 39
  reconciling with after
    abortion 114
  the unbaptized foetus 126–7
  Vatican II 44

# INDEX OF NAMES AND SUBJECTS

Ross, Loretta 76
rubella (German measles)
  abortion and 83, 85–9
  changed attitudes 106–7
  vaccine for 87

sacrifice, women's 119–21
Salvation Army 36
Samaritan, the Good 120–1
Sanger, Martha 36
Sarah, fertility of 4
Schlesinger, Eugene 120
Scotland, legal abortion in 42
sex
  Christian virtues and 136
  coercive/forced 54, 70
  commodification of 23
  for conception 115
  consent to pregnancy? xxi
  as consent to pregnancy 54–5
  contraception and 36
  disapproval of premarital 1
  forced or unconsented xxiii
  marital pleasure and 27
  marital procreation 10–11
  naturalness of 16–17
  outside marriage 17, 47
  pleasure and xviii
  promiscuity 40
  punishment for crimes of 15–16
  shifting Christian views on 14–19
  as sinful 13–14
  virginity and continence xviii

  without love 55
  Witte's list of crimes 15
sex education
  access to 76
  inadequate xxii
  inequalities xix
  language for discussion 23
sexism 131
sex selection 94
sexually-transmitted diseases,
  condoms and 36
sin
  anti-abortion stance ix
  language of xxii
  perception of judgement xi
  sex as xviii, 13–14
  talk 114–21
SisterSong 46, 76
society
  class and 40
  influences of 117
sodomy, as a crime 15
*Something to Celebrate:*
  *Valuing Families in Church*
  *and the Society* (Church of
  England) 17
'Sometimes It's a Child and a
  Choice' (Ludlow) xx
Song of Songs: the unfaithful
  wife 7
Sower, Parable of 11
Spiers, Archdeacon Pete 82–3
spina bifida
  folic acid and 80, 97
  prenatal screening 91
sports, disabled 107

Stapleton, Greg 94–5, 97, 100
Steel, David, Abortion Act and 26, 41
stem-cell research 44, 50
Stevenson-Moessner, Jeanne 120
stillbirth
  development problems 80
  loss and grief 64, 106
Stone, Howard W.
  *How to Think Theologically* (with Duke) xvi
Szreter, Simon 35–7

thalidomide
  abortion and 83, 84–9
  changed attitudes 106–7
Thecla 9
*Trust Women* (Peters) 139–40
Turner (Edward) syndrome 91

ultrasound scans 91–2
*The Unborn Bodies* (Kamitsuka) 127
United Kingdom
  Abortion Act, 1967 28, 44, 50, 88, 92
  abortion as illegal 27–8
  abortion saves lives 44–5
  abstinence as contraception 35–6
  attitudes towards abortion x
  baby loss certificate 64, 124
  deprivation and abortion 135
  legalizes abortion 26, 39–41
  maternal age 96
  mothers with other children 71
  NHS support for disabilities 103
  Offences Against the Person Act 34, 42, 45, 49
  outlawing abortion 33–4
  prenatal screening 90
  thalidomide and 84
United States
  abortion and disabilities 89
  Humane Abortion Act, California 88–9
  Infant Life Preservation Act 34
  legalizes abortion 28–9, 89
  maternal mortality 45
  mothers with other children 71
  outlawing abortion 33, 34–5, 46, 49
  pastoral care for abortion xii
  recent abortion restrictions 89
  Roe vs Wade 29
  strict anti-abortion laws 50–1
  thalidomide and 84, 86

*The Vindication of the Rights of Women* (Wollstonecraft) 16
virginity *see* chastity

# INDEX OF NAMES AND SUBJECTS

Williams, Rowan 21
Winner, Lauren 115
Witte, John 15–16
Wollstonecraft, Mary
  *The Vindication of the Rights of Women* 16
women
  assessing responsibility 134–5
  careers and pregnancy 20, 58
  chastity before marriage 5
  compassion for 137–8
  consequences of pregnancy 22
  controlling 54–5
  decisions and xiv–xv
  depiction in Christianity 2–23
  education of 16
  historical struggles 48
  individual situations of 138–41
  justifying decisions 129
  lacking support 135–6
  limited by motherhood 41
  maternal deaths 40, 41
  men's trust/control 3–7
  as morally weaker 22–3
  moral value of foetus 130–1
  motherhood vocation 131
  older mothers 102
  ordination of 16
  other children and 71
  power relations with men xxii
  prejudging experiences xi
  responsibility for decision 122–3
  sacrifices 119–21
  saying no 20
  social and religious views of 118
  stigma 55
  support for disabled children 103–4
  as temptresses 22–3
  theologians 139
  traditional Christianity and 19–23
  value of liturgy and prayers 130
  wandering wombs 7
*Women on the Web* 45
World Health Organization (WHO) 45

www.ingramcontent.com/pod-product-compliance
Lightning Source LLC
Chambersburg PA
CBHW022012290426
44109CB00015B/1147